To.

THE TEACHER'S /

YOU ARE CREATING SIGNIFICANCE IN THE
WAY IN WHICH YOU ARE DECIDING
KIDS TO BE LEADER. DON'T STOP! DON'T
SETTLE. BE A DISRUPTIVE INNOVATOR.

THE MIND AGE™:

MASTERING YOUR
INFINITE MIND
FOR SUCCESS

Love

Leeann

JAN 15

LEEANN C. NAIDOO

THE
MIND AGE™

Mastering your infinite mind for success
for 2040 and beyond

R3THINK PRESS

First published in Great Britain 2014
by Rethink Press (www.rethinkpress.com)

To my father, Ramamurthi 'Sonny' Naidoo, a modern day Leonardo da Vinci – thank you for inspiring life's greatest gift in me: a belief that anything is possible if I put my mind to it *and* if I act on it immediately.

To my mother, Rosalind Joan Naidoo my greatest teacher – thank you for instilling in me the discipline of working at something until I mastered it.

To my life partner, Shakeer Mahomed – thank you for being an infinite source of encouragement, for being my biggest fan and my greatest annoyance all at once. I want to believe you when you say that you are meant to bring out the worst in me so that only the best is left!

You have been my life's greatest influencers – thank you for making this dream come true!

CONTENTS

INTRODUCTION

I am the youngest of four children in a family of teachers: my now retired dad, my eldest sister Lyn (thirteen years older than I am), and my brother Trevor (eight years older than I am), are all members of this illustrious profession; while my sister Debbie (ten years older than I am) lectured for a while too. Although not professionally qualified, Mum is also one of the greatest teachers on the planet, able to teach anything with great success.

When I was born we lived in a suburb called Chatsworth on the outskirts of Durban, a seaside town on the east coast of South Africa created especially for Indians during the apartheid years. Chatsworth was and still is a far from glamorous suburb, although I would argue that Durban has some of the best beaches in the world. I loved every minute of being in Chatsworth. I had the best times of my life on Road 745, playing with the neighbourhood kids who are very much family to this day.

Life was quite simple then and I would probably have continued living a simple life, had it not been for my brother Trevor. He would do two things that would irritate me. From when I was about three (and he was eleven), he would wait for me to be in earshot and then discuss with my mum, in a very serious and hushed tone, the problem of my big feet. This went on for years. The second thing he would do, this time *out* of earshot from mum, was rap his knuckles over my head, cock his head to one side listening, then confirm that my head still sounded empty; that regrettably, as the youngest in the family, I had lost out, I hadn't made the cut and was brainless! One day he surprised me by saying, 'Wait! I can hear something. Listen!' He rapped my head sharply. 'I can hear a rattle,' he said. 'It's small, but it's there. Hurray! You have a pea brain at last. We just need to fix your big feet next and you'll be normal!' And with that he skipped off. I remember feeling slightly relieved but equally annoyed.

Fast forward through the next three decades of my life and my fascination with the brain and the mind took over. All thanks to Trevor, I guess. My circumstances, my experiences and the conditions of life generally around me ignited a desire in me to make a sustainable difference: to people, animals, the environment, and the planet, one step at a time, one person at a time.

What I saw around me and what I experienced personally, a lot of which is captured in this book, both inspired and hurt me a lot, which fuelled my motivation to want to do something about it. All my studying, reading, talking to people and working with brilliant minds led me to explore what the future might hold and I began questioning whether we are applying our minds effectively to build the best future possible.

This book is the result of my journey so far: my failings in life, my findings from the research I have done, deep personal stories and a perspective on what we need to do differently in the next 25 years to 2040, not just to survive, but to maximise happiness and success.

The signs are already evident, and my research confirms that the next 25 years, in particular, are going to be the most challenging ever. Whilst everybody, irrespective of age, really should be gearing up for this, it is my belief that we're not – because we're too busy, too tired, too stressed, have our own baggage to deal with, don't have money, believe that it's somebody else's problem to fix, or we choose to live in blissful ignorance of the inevitable.

We have come through the Ice Age, the Stone Age, the Iron Age, the Atomic Age, the Space Age, and most recently the Information Age. For the exponential change the world will go through in the coming decades, we are well and truly in the 'Mind Age™', in which it is entirely the mastery of the mind and heightened use of our brains that will enable us to be fully prepared for the 2040s – a date sufficiently far away but significantly close on the horizon for people like me, 40-something year olds. It also is a period of relevance for the generation before me as they redefine what retirement means for them, as well as for the generation just after, as they will need to make significant adjustments to career choices and progression, raising families and financial planning.

Irrespective of which generation you belong to, it all starts now.

The Mind Age™: Mastering your Infinite Mind for Success is about the present and the future. It is about accessing, unleashing then harnessing the power of your mind in a way that you may not have considered before – through the lens of what the world will look like by 2040 (Chapter 1). This is not a fluffy book. It draws on extensive research that is vitally important to set the context for what we need to start doing from now to be ready for that future (Chapter 2). The 8-E Model (Chapter 3 onwards) describes the attributes, all coincidentally beginning with the letter 'E', that are needed to create a paradigm shift in our lives. Incorporating neuroscience-based principles, each 'E' describes what needs to be developed and how, both in yourselves and in the people around you, in order to create a life of success, purpose and fulfilment. The 8-E Chapters define and describe how to: 'Envision' your best future, encourage 'Enquiring' minds to create breakthroughs in life, accelerate entrepreneurial innovation by developing 'Enterprising' behaviours, enhance 'Expertise' through alternative education, engage the world with evolved 'Emotional' skills, use your Environment as a springboard for positive change, exercise your brain to 'Energise' your mind, and finally 'Enrol' people in your endeavours so as to create echoes of positive change in the world.

One of the greatest pitfalls of books like these is that while focusing on what needs doing, they sometimes neglect the 'how' to do it and the 'how' to keep at it. Each chapter of the 8-Es goes into detail about the 'what', the 'so-what', the 'why', the 'who said so' and the 'how'.

It doesn't matter what your life situation is now. You may be a single mum, someone who has been out of work for a long time or whose self-esteem and self-worth may be ebbing away; perhaps you are someone struggling to make ends meet, someone who lacks focus; someone who feels like something's missing or you want more; someone who has been settling for mediocrity. Maybe you are in a good space – perhaps you are a student, someone at the peak of your career, someone contemplating a life change, someone who is curious or ambitious and wants to live their best life possible.

Whatever situation you are faced with, my hope is that this book helps you recognise what you need to do to secure a comfortable future.

I want this book to be a call to action, so I've drawn on the work of over 60 leading thinkers, authors and academics in the subjects of strategy, neuroscience, psychology, medical science, environmental conservation, business, leadership, and education. I have interviewed academics, CEOs, leading management consultants and heads of Human Resources & Talent in some of the world's top organisations; and brought together different perspectives from a variety of people, focus groups and workshops that I ran, so that the book as a whole speaks to each of us on different levels.

I have also drawn on my 20 years of business experience, working internationally for top consulting firms where I managed large scale, complex transformation programmes of major organisations. As a specialist in change, I incorporate over 30 methods, models, strategies and frameworks when coaching executives, business professionals, entrepreneurs and students, which I've shared to an extent in here. I've included principles from psychology through to neuroscience, guaranteed to deliver high impact and sustainable results. I've also shared several deeply personal events in my life, which I hope you will be able to relate to and which I hope inspire you to take charge of your life and redefine your destiny.

I hope this book compels you to act immediately. To help with this I've developed a decision-making model in Chapter 9: Enrolment, to accelerate you to your 'tipping point', to make that decision that changes your life for the best. This is the one time when doing the same things or doing nothing are no longer options. I am optimistic that this book will ignite that part of you which hungrily seeks to develop your mind, and does not entirely leave it to science and business to discover or dictate who or what we should be.

'The best way to predict your future is to create it'
PETER DRUCKER.

I personally do not want the future thrust upon me, nor do I want to race to catch up with the future. I don't want to inherit my future. I want to be a part of shaping and influencing it. I want to know what's coming. I want to know how much is enough to prepare for it. I want to know that I am doing the right things in the right order and the right quantities. I think you may want the same.

'Change will not come if we wait for some other person or some other time. We are the ones we've been waiting for. We are the change that we seek,'
BARACK OBAMA

ONE

ABOUT THE FUTURE

'Someone is sitting in the shade today because
someone planted a tree a long time ago,'
WARREN BUFFETT (BORN 1930)

To say that the world is undergoing an exponential change would be an understatement. The last 25 years have seen remarkable changes in technology, healthcare, education and business, and this trend will continue at an even greater pace over the next 25 years and beyond. Here are my thoughts, backed by a wide range of research and reinforced by interviews with business leaders, on what the future will look like. The future starts with people.

Population growth

Between the years 1800 and 1950, the UN estimated the world population to have grown from 1 billion to 2.5 billion people. Between 1950 and 2012 that number grew to approximately 7 billion, believed to have been reached somewhere between October 2011 and March 2012 as stated by the UN Population Fund and the US Census Bureau respectively. By 2040 that number could climb to approximately 9 billion people, according to a report published by the United Nations Department of Economic and Social Affairs, called the *World Population Prospects*. It highlights that the population of developed regions will remain largely unchanged at around 1.3 billion from now until 2050. In contrast, the 49 least developed countries in the world are projected to double in size from around 900 million people in 2013 to 1.8 billion by 2050. The report notes that the population of India is expected to exceed China's around 2028, and after that India's population will continue to grow while China's will be expected to start decreasing, largely due to the one child policy.

Overall, life expectancy is projected to increase in developed and developing countries in future years. At a global level, it is projected to reach 76 years in the period 2045-2050 and 82 years by 2095-2100. By the end of the century, people in developed countries could live on average up to 89 years, compared to about 81 years in developing regions. A consequence of the ageing population is that state pension budgets will continue to bear strain meaning an overall decreased income for senior citizens. Retirement ages will have to be pushed out in America, Asia and most European countries, where many people will be forced to work into their 70s. The impact on the health of the population will be severe, with stress increasing phenomenally and depression likely to be the biggest killer by the 2040s.

There is of course an argument that a shift in consciousness or a change in the natural order of life will alter the birth or fertility rates around the world, thereby causing a decline in population growth. A perspective by Jørgen Randers, a Norwegian professor of climate strategy at the Norwegian Business School, and practitioner in the field of future studies, argues that traditional projections do not adequately consider fertility factors and therefore estimates a *'most likely scenario of a peak in the world population in the early 2040s at about 8.1 billion people, followed by a decline.'*

One child policies are questionable as a solution to the population explosion. Licensing and regulations are accepted practices to qualify for driving a car or piloting an aeroplane, and we are under intense scrutiny when applying to adopt a child or a pet, yet paradoxically people are free to produce as many children as they choose, despite their ability to take care of them adequately. Some cultures 'count' children as wealth, blessings from God, and status symbols in their communities. Not bearing children in these cultures leaves couples open to criticism, rejection and even exorcism, where infertility is perceived as a sign from God or possession by evil spirits. In many countries, governments provide grants for each child born into a financially disadvantaged family. Whilst there are many deserving people out there who benefit from this, there are abusers of the system who use this income stream as a substitute for earning an honest living. The impact is that governments need to invest heavily to address problems in the system. The exponential growth in population will have a phenomenal impact on life as we know it and policies such as these will not be sustainable in many countries by the 2040s.

Consequently, housing, sanitation, waste disposal, education, healthcare, energy provision, nutrition, technology, transportation, communication, crime detection, security and safety will also be impeded, calling for radical solutions to already substandard provisioning. An increase in the number of people in an already overcrowded space with sparse facilities is bound to increase the crime rate, although in the future I don't believe this will be the case in all countries. I came to that conclusion based on reviewing trends over the last three decades, and my work with various police forces in the UK in recent years.

I believe that by the 2040s, despite many people being out of work, depression being rife, social aid not at all what it should be and competition for skills high, crime statistics and violent crime in particular will be at its lowest. The reason is quite simply because by then detection will be at its most sophisticated. Much of my work with police forces in the UK focused on forensics, mobile access to information, and improved case file management. Many innovative solutions were at that time already being trialled: for example, increased use of facial and body recognition systems, instantaneous analysis of evidence using portable devices achieved through the integration of smart technologies and utilising powerful search engine capability that accessed cloud networks. Further into the future it is hoped that Google Glass type devices will enable data collection by scanning the environment like a video camera would, but with more sophisticated functionality that analyses features of the environment, e.g. calculating heights, defining textures of solid material, recording critical information relevant to a crime scene, to name but a few features. Imprisonment will decline greatly, partly because sophisticated detection will act as a deterrent, but mostly because different incarceration methods will be adopted alongside medical advances aiding rehabilitation.

No matter what the rules, or what governmental policies and societal norms evolve into, and irrespective of the exact number of the future population, it's safe to say that there will be an increase in the number of people on the planet in the next few decades; with it come challenges and opportunities. So before the critics amongst you get lost in the debate about the actual number or the scale of the impact, we need to acknowledge that our planet is already struggling to cope with the existing population challenges. The environment is being abused every day. We are already experiencing a decrease in landmass due to the melting icebergs and rising water levels. Add another 2 billion people to the planet by 2040 doing the same things we are doing now, and what happens then?

We need to explore new avenues to sustain human life. We need new thinking, strategists and idea generators. We need space.

Space colonisation

With space on earth limited, advances in space travel will inevitably develop. Space colonisation pioneers and scientists, like the now late Gerard O'Neill, proposed ideas for human settlement in space. Stephen Hawking, the theoretical physicist and cosmologist, in more recent years stated that mankind faces the option of either colonising space within the next two hundred years and building residential units on other planets, or face the prospect of long-term extinction.

Whether we are faced with a gradual decline in Earth's resources, or whether there is a catastrophic impact to Earth's biosphere, there will inevitably be a need to create an alternative habitat. Currently there is a drive for leisure travel into space, and this trend is growing with the endeavours of people like Elon Musk, Dennis Tito and Richard Branson.

South-African-born Elon Musk is the CEO and CTO of SpaceX, CEO & Chief Product Architect of Tesla Motors, and founder of PayPal. What makes him noteworthy is that he regularly launches rockets into space via his commercial spaceflight company SpaceX Corp, which also delivers supplies to the International Space Station using its Dragon Spacecraft. Dennis Tito, engineer and multimillionaire, most famously known as the first space tourist to have funded his own trip to space in 2001, is interested in collaborating with Musk for his 2018 flyby of Mars. Add Richard Branson's Virgin Galactic space programme to the mix, running passenger flights into space, and we suddenly have the beginnings of this reality.

Think about the evolution of this journey. Leisure space travel will evolve into the development of temporary habitable accommodation, which in turn will evolve to more permanent accommodation, and will eventually include all the amenities we enjoy here – and then some. This creates the need for a whole ecosystem to support this industry – space flight travel agents, hoteliers, estate agents, financial services, employment opportunities, utilities providers. Are we gearing up for this already? Are we educating for these skills? Take one of the elements of this ecosystem, for example utilities. Initially they will need to fly resources to the colony but eventually they will need to look at self-sustaining energy sources, and waste disposal solutions. Flying waste back to Earth is not an option, if I get to have it my way, neither is dumping waste in space despite the attraction of black holes! The Kessler Syndrome, a chain-reaction of collisions between orbital technologies (e.g. satellites) and debris, best describes the scenario where waste accumulates over time, the volume and density of that waste causes collisions, generating further debris, which causes a cascade effect of additional collisions. This in turn could render space exploration and the use of satellites unfeasible and even life on Earth could be threatened if objects breached the atmosphere.

The leisure industry attraction aside, with energy reserves likely to be exhausted on Earth by the 2040s, opportunities to mine near-Earth asteroids will become an attractive business proposition, since many of these asteroids are estimated to contain more metal than exists on Earth. It is also anticipated that water may be available in abundance. Recognising the huge revenue potential, many new companies will form, specialising in particular technologies, spacecraft and mining methods. Banish the thought, however, of a NASA-looking astronaut in a space suit controlling a huge jack-hammer on a hurtling rock in space – the image is more likely to be highly sophisticated robotics, automated probes, self-guided heavy machinery and advanced shielding.

So that's the giant leap to be taken from here to there. And with this comes the very real need for innovative solutions. Are we investing enough in this new area – financially and intellectually? We need to create the environment in which these solutions can be developed.

The environment

Rachel Carson was seen by many as the pioneer of the green movement in the 1930s. Backed by a prestigious career, her book, *Silent Spring*, published in 1962, brought to life the damage done by the incessant use of pesticides. It caused uproar amongst politicians at the time, but her work ignited the idea that we are part of a life-sustaining eco-system. Sir David Attenborough has also brought natural history into our living rooms for over 50 years, highlighting the profound impact we have on the environment around us. Environmental organisations such as Greenpeace, Friends of the Earth, World Wide Fund for Nature (WWF), the European Environmental Agency (EEA) and others continue their philanthropic journeys to improve the plight of the planet, imploring us to do more to achieve a paradigm shift in environmental sustainability.

Before attempting to fix the problem, however, it is important to understand its origins. Approximately 300 million years ago, much of the atmospheric carbon was converted into inert material such as coal and other fossils, but has been released in recent years by the burning of high volumes of coal, oil, and natural gas.

Excessive CO_2 becomes problematic because its transparency allows the sun's rays to enter the earth's atmosphere; the heat reflected back from the earth's surface is trapped and creates a greenhouse effect, thereby raising the global temperature.

If CO_2 levels continue to climb, the Arctic is predicted to become ice-free in the summer months of the 2040s, according to scientists at the US Centre for Atmospheric Research, permanently displacing wild-life, bird-life and human life. The release of methane from melting permafrost also compounds the situation, with more species of animals, birds and insects at risk of extinction. The shifts in atmospheric pressure and other related conditions will see an increase in the occurrence of volcanoes, earthquakes, and other extreme weather patterns.

Other activities that are currently impacting the environment are mining techniques such as horizontal drilling and hydraulic fracturing ('fracking') which will continue to radically transform the production of oil and gas. Environmentalists are firmly against fracking, claiming that the threat of methane leakage is high, as are the risks associated with disposing waste water. Fracking will also require industrial-style development causing environmental hazards and adverse effects on local communities. The good news, however, is that technological advancements are underway to clean up and treat the waste water.

Mining of oil shale from sedimentary rock containing kerogen is likely to continue to grow in popularity by the 2040s, since it can be used as a substitute for conventional crude oil. Even though extraction of the oil is currently more costly than producing crude oil, there are major deposits available around the world. Interest in shale is also growing as a possible transportation fuel that could one day replace petrol in certain types of vehicles. Sasol, a South African company, is in discussions to build an energy plant in the US that would convert gas to high-quality diesel.

Power stations in the US in particular are under constant pressure to switch to clean gas. Even the US nuclear industry is suffering. Competition from cheaper gas-generated power forced four nuclear plants to close in 2012.

In recent decades, environmental issues have risen to the top of political agendas, and rightly so. Al Gore and his efforts on environmental issues have helped this along somewhat. Still, there's a long journey ahead, and fortunately some clever minds are applying themselves to the solutions. Bill Gates, the Microsoft founder, has started up a new company called TerraPower, which turns nuclear waste into nuclear fuel while providing affordable, low-carbon electricity. Despite the bad press about nuclear energy, it is a proven source of reliable base-load power, and TerraPower's Travelling Wave Reactor (TWR) mitigates the concerns about safety, costs and environmental impact. The TWR uses inexpensive depleted uranium as fuel, only needing to replenish fuel stocks after 40 years, compared to traditional reactors that usually require refuelling every 18 months to two years. The company expects a prototype to be ready for demonstration and hopes to have a commercial reactor up and running in the 2020s.

Bill Gates and his team of scientists and engineers believe global energy demand will grow by 70+% consumed by the 9 billion-strong population between 2030 and 2040. ExxonMobil in their '*Outlook for Energy: A View to 2040*' Report (2014), estimate that about 60% of the world's demand for energy will be supplied by oil and natural gas, with a 90% growth in demand for electricity.

Innovation is seen to be growing in this sector, although it is questionable whether deep water drilling and mining operations will continue into the future, given the number of ecological disasters and spills in recent years and the pressures that governments are imposing on safety and risk standards. Spills such as BP's Deepwater Horizon rig (approximately 200 million gallons) in 2010 and the Ixtoc I oil well (approximately 140 million gallons) in 1979, both in the Gulf of Mexico, and the deliberate spill caused by Iraqi troops during the Gulf War to prevent American troops from landing (approximately 520 million gallons) in 1991, all remain imprinted on our emotional canvasses as something we hope will never be repeated.

That being said with depleting resources, many organisations are still keen to continue with deep water mining, investing significantly in this area.

For the innovation required in the environment we live in, we need energy.

Energy

Currently oil prices are sending the costs of energy globally through the roof. Coupled with the demands of a growing population, this has put huge strain on the world's power grids. In regions like South Africa 'load shedding' has been implemented since the late 2000s, as there is not enough electricity available to consumers via the electricity provider. Households have become more aware of their consumption and have actively taken measures to cut back. Antiquated infrastructure in South Africa and in many other countries has not helped either, with a large percentage of electricity being lost during production, transmission and utilisation.

Power grids will improve to include smart sensors within them to regulate the flow of electricity. Bi-directional flow will ensure that 'unused' electricity can be sent back into the system, making for more efficient usage. It is anticipated that in time regions will integrate their grids on a country-to-country basis, making for a web of energy provision. *'Infrastructure is expensive to build and maintain. The winners will be those that can integrate different network infrastructures globally,'* says Douglas Umbers, MD and leader of world class, technology enabled, service organisations.

For these and other solutions to be developed, we need to create a hunger for people to want to change, a thirst to sustain change and a desire to commit to its sustainability.

Water and food

With a 30% population growth expected by 2040, it is safe to assume that we will need a more than 30% increase in water provisioning, since many parts of the world still do not have access to fresh supplies. The only problem with needing more water in future is that fresh water supplies will be close to, if not already, exhausted by then, placing huge pressure on the speed at which desalination of seawater and containerisation is being managed.

We are faced with quite a dilemma – decreasing fresh water supplies, yet the melting icebergs are adding volumes of fresh water to sea levels causing them to rise. In the 1990s, Greenland's ice mass remained stable; however in recent years its ice sheet has declined rapidly. As Greenland holds 10% of the total global ice mass, if it were to melt, according to the Natural Resources Defence Council, sea levels could increase by up to 21 feet, wiping out most islands and low-lying countries.

Are you ready for the reefs of the future? The once majestic architecture of the 21st century soon to be crumbling high-rises, remnants of collapsed freeways and other rotting building structures peeking out of the sea as you drive by – a consequence of increased CO_2 levels, melting icebergs and rising sea levels.

We need radical advances in providing fresh water for the future. Desalination of water meaning the extraction of salt from seawater, will be required on a large scale in future. In addition it will need to consume lower energy for it to efficiently become the world's primary source of freshwater. Already Middle-Eastern countries have invested in desalination plants. Jebel Ali is the largest plant in the UAE, whilst up to 50% of Israel's domestic water consumption comes from desalinated seawater.

Another strategy that is currently being considered to address the hybrid electricity-water production issue described above, involves compact, floating 'energy islands'. Early models of this showed a hexagonally shaped structure, interlocked with other islands, forming artificial archipelagos. Wind turbines and concentrated solar power are installed on the topsides – while on the undersides, flash-evaporated seawater is used to drive turbine generators, which in turn will produce drinkable water.

These combine offshore power generation with desalination plants and could also include other forms of energy such as wave, wind, sea currents and solar energy. First demonstrated in the 2010s, more of these energy islands could be deployed in coastal areas which enjoy optimal conditions for ocean thermal energy conversion (OTEC).

A harsh warning, reported by the *Guardian* newspaper in 2012, from leading water scientists, said that the world may have to switch to a vegetarian diet for the next 40 years to avoid the catastrophic shortage in global food supplies. There is not enough water for the croplands, to feed the animals as well as produce additional food for the extra 2 billion people expected to be on the planet from 2040 onwards.

Humans currently obtain approximately 20% of their protein intake from animal-based products, but this may have to drop to 5% by then to feed the extra 2 billion people, as it is estimated that there will be just enough water if the proportion of animal foods is limited to 5%. At the moment, 900 million people go hungry and over 2 billion people are malnourished. That is the world we have created today. Add another 2 billion people.

Are you ready for this new world?

Water is a necessity of human life, and without food we will perish. We need new skills to come up with the solution to providing fresh water. We need to move on it.

Transport

As a result of the fuel challenge, most new vehicles produced in future will be electric cars that will need to be recharged or they will be hybrids. We already have the technology for self-driving cars today, but we lack the infrastructure and mind-set to make them work properly, so it will be interesting to see the extent to which high population growth, lack of space and the energy crisis accelerate the introduction of these innovations.

Cars today already have emergency braking systems, self-parking and freeway cruising features, but the next breakthrough in vehicles will be the enhanced use of smart technologies that enable self-drive features, adapting to changing road and weather conditions.

Manufacturers will have a huge role to play guaranteeing safety standards of their vehicles, and insurers will need to continue investing in sophisticated technologies to make claims indisputable. As you can see, this becomes an industry in itself. Discovery Insurance in South Africa is a good example of this, where they install a 'tracker' device on all vehicles they insure, which monitors the driving patterns of the drivers, tracks speed, and can even deduce whether someone was texting whilst driving!

Are the current generations aware of these developments, and are we doing enough to develop the requisite interest and skills to contribute ideas and solutions to these professions?

It is my view, that as the population grows, more people will flock to cities for the perceived promise of employment. Demands on the transport system will increase, making mass transport more attractive, but at the same time demanding efficient and reliable service. Technological advances and improved safety features will mean that the very fastest train routes will be comparable to flying times. We will also see rail systems from Europe, India, Russia and Japan linking up. In an effort to address future capacity needs, improve service reliability and reduce travel times, Amtrak as an example has formulated plans for a $117 billion, 30-year investment program in constructing a high-speed rail (HSR) route, along America's North East Corridor, with trains running at up to 220 mph (354 kph), with improved reliability and greater capacity. More HSR networks are planned for the next few decades such as China's HSR, California's HSR, and the UK's Scotland to London service.

Are we ready for this new era in transportation? Are we encouraging the interest in upcoming generations? Are we educating appropriately? Will we be able to employ people with the right skills so as to create superior solutions for our needs at that time?

Employment

Employment models will continue to change but at a more staggering rate. An influx of people to city centres seeking employment will create a demand for better facilities such as education and healthcare, putting pressure on the system.

However, as organisations face continued cost pressures, the size of their operations will drastically reduce to a lean workforce, keeping only essential business functions and critical skills in-house whilst outsourcing the rest, not to third party suppliers as has been done over the last two decades, but to the free market. If technology has exponentially advanced enough to hold all the necessary personal data and will execute traditional HR and remuneration functions, 'people management practices' will become a non-event. It will therefore make more sense to contract directly with the market, as it subtracts the unnecessary overhead of 'management fees' charged by outsourced providers.

The future will see a greater use of virtual employees as well as virtual automated 'employees' based on interactive software. Antiquated versions of these have been used as far back as the 1990s – activated by simple voice commands – but many organisations experiencing high call volumes, such as cinemas and banks, have implemented more sophisticated interactive voice technologies to assist with basic customer queries, while real people will need to engage with customers on more complex issues.

Greater use of technology will redefine employment models. Even outsourced providers will be greatly affected – not only will we see them reduce in number but their service offerings will also radically change, if not disappear completely. Not even specialist, large-scale operations like data centres will survive, as cloud computing will have completely revolutionised how we store, access and retrieve high volumes of even confidential data.

Marc Kahn, Head of Human Resources & Organisation Development at Investec Bank in South Africa, told me that he has taken a rather unconventional view by creating an internal recruitment team who 'originate talent into the bank'. They do this by approaching people in other organisations who are not actively looking to change jobs. By 'attracting' them into his organisation, he believes he is therefore recruiting the best of the best, making for more productive placements and greater employee engagement – critical factors in creating the next generation workforce. Marc believes future changes to banking will include phasing out the credit card. Going forward, biometric methods such as finger prints and iris scans will be used to track personal credit and, whilst there is still a long way to go, cash will disappear. Despite the huge move toward digitisation, this will still not remove the personal element to banking – money is an emotive issue, and so people will need to transact with people in banking environments for more complex issues.

'There's no doubt in my mind. There is an absolute, unbridled race on to achieve digital efficiency. Leaders who are able to lead in the Digital age, whilst ensuring that human interaction is a differentiator, will be the winners. Going forward it's going to be about relationships and meaning.'

MARC KAHN, 2014

Despite the technological advances, a number of call centres, for example T-Mobile's 'Everything Everywhere' operation, have recently brought 'customer care' back on-shore. Customers fed back that they wanted to speak to someone who related better to them. A familiar accent helps, but might another consideration be that we need to re-evaluate our hiring practices of older people? Might older people in service centres be a voice customers can trust? This is certainly a view that is championed by Douglas Umbers, MD and leader of world class, technology-enabled, service organisations, who shared in an interview with me that,

> 'An ageing population creates new opportunities and potentially exciting employment models that give new value to the individuals, organisations and to wider society. It more than addresses the global pensions crisis, and it provides stimulation and opportunity for able-bodied older people. It's a must for the future!'

Andrew Crossey, Senior Vice President and Global Talent Management Director of Capgemini, one of the largest Consulting, Technology and Outsourcing firms in the world, told me,

> 'The best people will be in demand. We will see a significant shift in employment models: more freelancing and multiple employments will radically transform the employment landscape. As a result, I see a merging of 'eBay' and 'LinkedIn' conceptually. The best people will set out their stall and organisations will bid for their services. Whereas present day corporations advertise roles at set salary bands, in future we will see more of a shift to individuals and groups of people developing solutions to business problems, targeting specific organisations, driving up competition and ultimately selling to the highest bidder.'

If this is true, we are also likely to see many jobs disappear. Manufacturing will see a huge decline in interest as automation takes over critical functions. Farming is also headed that way, despite the challenges described earlier regarding food production. We need more clever minds to come up with both the recipe and the menu for food production in the future. With some jobs disappearing, new jobs will be created. As I muse over the anticipated developments of the future merged with some of my favourite science fiction books and movies, I wonder whether a 'Memory Augmentation Surgeon' will really be able to implant a memory chip into a human brain to upload / download various skills, information, knowledge or perhaps even virtual memories. I wonder what jetlag will feel like for a Space Tour Guide, and whether Body Part Makers would come up with more creative job titles!

Changes to employment models, new ways of working and new skills requirements have far-reaching ramifications on several aspects of our lives. Firstly what exactly are we educating for? How are educational institutions researching and then gearing up for the upcoming changes? Secondly, are we opening doors and encouraging the next generation to explore new opportunities or are we influencing them to improve only incrementally on what we've been able to achieve? Which professions are we punting and why? Will the professions that we are in now still exist in the same capacity as they are now by the 2040s?

Thinking the whole process through, financial planning and wealth creation for our future becomes that much more difficult – our chances of being employed by organisations will be radically reduced since only specialists and therefore the minority of the population, who are knowledgeable in a variety areas and not just one, will receive regular monthly incomes. Company benefits will be limited to the privileged few, pensions savings will reach a whole new level as older people work for longer, and, as the majority of the population will be unable to rely on steady employment income, they will need to create their own income streams, with passive and residual income streams becoming ever more crucial.

What we need is a new perspective on business, employment, skills and outputs. We need to think ahead. We need to think globally.

Globalisation

Globalisation is a collective term that is used to describe a combination of elements such as global economics, the trading of commodities, mobility of people across various geographies and the transference of knowledge, all of which are affected primarily by business and socio-cultural norms. The rapid increase in cross-border movement of goods, services, technology and capital has led to the emergence of a global marketplace and greater interdependence between various economies.

Focusing specifically on the people implications of globalisation, it is safe to assume several things. Despite major advances in tele- and video-conferencing, other remote working capabilities, and organisational cultures evolving to accommodate a variety of flexible workforce arrangements, critical business will still be done in person, business deals will be closed in person, and project start-ups will kick off in person. There will still very much need to be an in-person dynamic to business. Technology will not entirely replace the need for face-to-face contact at critical stages of business lifecycles. Therefore, we need to ensure that we create global leaders and global workers for the future.

The extreme demands of globalisation require a new generation of people who are immediately mobile yet have the strength of character to manage numerous virtual workers and teams. As organisations continue to downscale, the increased demands of jobs, the varied working hours, the challenges that each of us will be expected to overcome, the complexity of problems that we will be required to solve, and the wide and deep nature of work itself will take its toll on employees. They will be expected to produce greater outputs by processing higher volumes of information, recalling efficiently, synthesising rapidly, and articulating concisely. Better memories and vocal eloquence will be a must.

A major study by the Organisation for Economic Co-operation and Development (OECD), reported by the BBC in Oct 2013, shows how England's 16 to 24-year-olds are falling behind their Asian and European counterparts in literacy and mathematics. England ranked 22nd for literacy and 21st for numeracy out of 24 countries, accompanied by the US ranking 24th for numeracy. The top five countries excelling in numeracy include the Netherlands, Finland, Japan, Belgium and South Korea. We cannot become a world where the newer generations are less capable than the older generations in critical skills.

Alan Richell, management consultant and specialist in developing Change Leadership in the UK and the Middle East, says that one of the key attributes of future leaders is to be

'an excellent communicator and orator, able to crystallise their message in a way that is insistent, consistent and persistent: insistent on demanding excellence of their people, consistent in their messages, and persistent in driving forward their vision.'

The challenge we are faced with is to encourage Generation Z (born in the 2000s) to develop an interest in mathematics, all the sciences, engineering and economics, to meet the demands of the global economy of the future. In addition, we need to balance the positive effects of messaging, gaming and mobile communications with developing engaging, charismatic and articulate leaders of the future. We need a productive and healthy lifestyle to achieve this.

Healthcare

The knock-on effect of a faster pace of life with higher demands and greater challenge is the impact on our health. The speed with which we work, the advances in communications and travel will in turn demand greater physical and mental agility. This leaves us at risk of burnout and becoming ill unless we cope with challenges better and indeed master how we deal with stress and conflict in more taxing environments.

Adopting a mind-set of avoidance or defeat will guarantee our failure as a species. Challenges will serve as great opportunities for those who adopt creative mind-sets and a desire to develop the solutions. If we adopt a positive attitude we are likely to see great advances in the area of healthcare. Nanoparticles, a new wave in technology, are already being incorporated into drugs, while other more advanced areas of nanotechnology are being tested in biomedical, optical and electronic fields. In the future, nano-robots, ranging in size from 0.1–10 micrometres, are anticipated to make repairs on a cellular level, which when combined with the advances in stem cell research, will revolutionise the way we detect and treat damage and disease in the human body. It would not therefore be too much of a stretch of the imagination to believe that cancers will be eradicated, poor eye-sight reversed and mental illness will be fully treatable.

With that being the revolutionary path, direct technology interfaces with the human brain will soon become the norm. Human-technology interfaces are already beginning to have many practical applications in the world of business (e.g. virtual classrooms, blended learning), in the fields of medicine (e.g. remote surgeries where surgeons in different locations of the world perform surgeries on patients using robotics and other sophisticated technology), and aviation (e.g. the use of flight simulators to train pilots on crisis management).

The key take-away from the advances in healthcare is simply this: irrespective of the pace of life in the future, irrespective of our ability to manage with and excel in the face of the demands that life will throw our way, and despite the advances in healthcare and medicine, one thing is certain, our brain has tremendous untapped potential. It is time to learn how to unleash its power. It is not up to the science world to make discoveries – it is up to each one of us to tap into our own brain and create not only the optimal level of health, but also the mind-set that is required to develop the healthcare solutions of the future.

Despite all the current day distractions of finding a job, keeping it, progressing within it, dealing with the challenges of our careers, running a business, balancing work and family, finding time for ourselves, travelling, managing financial pressures, taking care of ageing parents, supporting our children in school, securing financial assistance for a good education for them, enabling them to develop personal interests, develop skills in sport, music, the arts; despite how much we might care about the future, are we really doing enough?

I am not willing to accept a Malthusian catastrophe to regulate population through disease, starvation and war, as a means of coping! Are we ready for the faster pace, not just physically but emotionally too? If you knew now that what you are doing is just short or a lot short of securing your best future, would you go the extra mile? What would it take to make that change today?

Working as we do now, living as we do now, thinking as we do now, and being as we are now… it's not going to be enough to be ready for this new way of life! We need to start preparing for what we need for the future, and that starts from today.

So allow me to take you on a journey of self-discovery, challenge and intrigue, to not just create it, but to enjoy every minute of living your future now.

What do we need to be, do and have, to survive and thrive by 2040 and beyond?

There is an inordinate amount of change on the horizon. What you have read so far has been a mere snapshot of what some of the key elements could be. It might have felt somewhat depressing, overwhelming or even ridiculous at times, I know. My intention was to bring into focus specific areas of interest, so that we actively contribute to its development. Whether I've underestimated or overestimated is inconsequential to what needs to be done next. And what needs to be done next is simpler than you may think.

The brain has huge untapped potential. The mind, by my definition, is the higher order working of the brain, infusing conscious and unconscious aspects of thought, creativity, memory, emotion, perception. Mastery of the mind is what I believe is needed to create our best future, and what that does is puts our brain into a new gear.

To help assimilate the concept of Mastery of the Mind, I've broken it down into eight elements, called the 8-E Model, which, if actively developed, will also cultivate a remarkable life and a huge improvement to the planet.

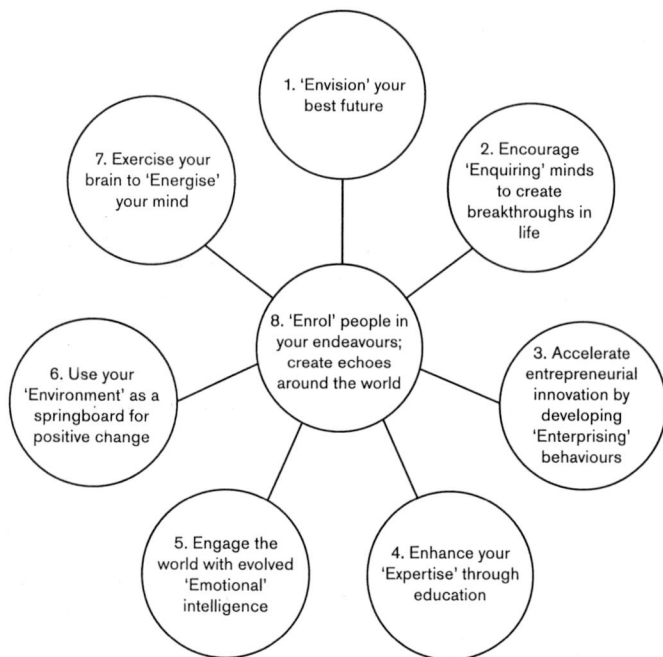

1. 'Envision' your best future
2. Encourage 'Enquiring' minds to create breakthroughs in life
3. Accelerate entrepreneurial innovation by developing 'Enterprising' behaviours
4. Enhance your 'Expertise' through education
5. Engage the world with evolved 'Emotional' intelligence
6. Use your 'Environment' as a springboard for positive change
7. Exercise your brain to 'Energise' your mind
8. 'Enrol' people in your endeavours; create echoes around the world

Each of these elements is a chapter that provides a definition of what that concept means, describes how to embark on making the change and outlines how to sustain it into the future. The first 'E' in the next chapter, called 'Envisioning your best future,' describes how a powerful vision magnetises you to the achievement of life goals, weaving a personal experience of mine into lessons that I hope you will benefit from too. 'Encouraging enquiring minds to create breakthroughs in life' shows how to create your own, and foster in others, a mind-set of curiosity to deal with life's challenges. My personal story of breakdowns and breakthroughs, undergoing massive personal change unfolds in 'accelerating entrepreneurial innovation by developing enterprising behaviours' which explores the attributes of successful entrepreneurs, adapting it to how this could be valuable in everyday life. 'Enhancing expertise through alternative education' provides ideas on how to build capability outside the box, so to speak; while 'Engaging the world with evolved emotional intelligence' provides my enhancement on Daniel Goleman's five constructs emotional intelligence model. The chapter on 'Using your environment as a springboard for positive change' adopts three perspectives, challenging you to accept the environment in which you started off from or that you are in right now, then encouraging you to create the environment that you need to thrive in despite your circumstances, and finally compelling you take a more active role in environmental preservation. 'Exercising your brain to energise your mind' is the chapter that follows, and continues with my personal journey, providing helpful ideas on energising your body and your mind. 'Enrolling people in your endeavours so as to create echoes of positive change in the world' explores a personally developed model on decision-making, its triggers, the role of emotions, and explains how collaboration (through enrolment) will be critically important for the future.

All of the chapters provide some insights into the brain, its mechanics and how to harness the power of your mind taking small, easy steps to eventually build 'mind muscle' to achieve those goals you dared to dream about.

The final chapter reveals my trigger and motivation for writing this book, and is something I know that everyone will be able to relate to. This deeply personal account of my life, as ordinary as it is, I hope will inspire you to extraordinary achievements.

'All that we are is the result of what we have thought.
The mind is everything. What we think, we become.'
BUDDHA (563 – 483BC)

TWO

ENVISION YOUR BEST FUTURE THAT FOCUSES AND DIRECTS EFFORT

'The only thing worse than being blind
is having sight but no vision'

HELEN KELLER (1880 – 1968)

I was 6 years old the very first time I began thinking about my vision for my life. It was the summer of 1981. I was due to start school in a few weeks. My first priority was to build a brain – Trevor made me believe that mine was smaller than everyone else's and apparently I would need it for school, so I had some work to do. My second priority was to use my brain somehow to reduce the size of my feet just in case someone noticed at school. My third priority was to marry a big guy to beat Trevor up one day. I had my sights set on my heartthrob Randolph Mantooth from the 1970s hit US TV series called *Emergency!*, but Mum said he would be too old by the time she would allow me to marry. This was a crushing blow to my life-plan as I had no concept of time at this age. My final priority was to source an endless supply of ice-cream, which I thought becoming a cashier one day (with that magically endless supply of cash flowing from their cash registers), would help me achieve. Mum set me straight on that too. Life was tough already!

Fortunately school came along two weeks later and life was great again. I worked hard on building my brain and putting my big feet to good use. I fed my brain with loads of ice-cream, information and knowledge, like a hoover sucks dust, reading everything I could possibly find everywhere I went. I won every sporting event I participated in and I was top of the class every academic year. By the time I got to high-school, my ice-cream yearnings subsided, and were replaced by needing to make a firm career decision. In South Africa, your choice of subjects in high school influences the course you can study at University, which in turn needs to correlate to your career choice. I realised that following my siblings in the teaching profession was not for me. I wore braces on my teeth in high school and I was very self-conscious of speaking. This led me to think that something back-office would be a good choice of career. I liked the idea of being a school secretary; I could speak on the phone, no one would see my teeth, I was a good typist, I could punch mean holes into paper that needed filing and I would benefit from half-days and loads of holidays working at a school. Sorted? No, not sorted. 'Our family does not produce secretaries!' Mum said sternly. The school secretary option was firmly off the table.

I studied the toughest course in high school, because Mum expected it and Dad would accept no less. Off I went to university, failed my first year, and saw Dad disappointed in me for the first time. It was clear he wasn't going to fund my second year. Debbie took pity and paid my fees – an opportunity to redeem myself!

I worked hard that year, studying nights and weekends as I worked a full time job, trying to prove to myself that I could do this. It paid off – I passed, and managed to secure a promotion working for an amazing woman, named Moira, who taught me all the essentials about management and leadership.

Dad helped me get set up in my first tiny apartment. Life was good, but hard work, I remember, not just the studying and working but I had to travel a lot too. Years seemed to fly by in a blur. I got married and the grind just continued. One day, Dad called. He and Mum had divorced a few years before that, and now recently retired and with Father's Day coming up, he said, 'You know how you always ask me what I want for Father's Day and I usually don't need anything? Well this year, I could really do with a new blanket please.'

'Sure,' I replied. Great that I'd be able to do something for him, I thought.

The next day I swiped my card at the cashier to pay for the blanket I'd picked out from Dad's favourite store, and my card was declined. Twice. As was the other card. Conversations with my bank manager later that afternoon got me nowhere. I had exceeded all credit limits, and was way overdrawn, he said. Apparently I had been in this situation for seven months in a row and hadn't realised it. It was the 12th of the month, payday felt like eons away, and I was seriously broke. I couldn't afford a blanket! Suddenly I realised that it was more than just a blanket. There was no money for food or petrol to get to work. That realisation opened the floodgates! I was 23, I was unhappily married, and I had nowhere to turn, having exhausted all credit options and having asked my sisters too many times for help.

I felt that I had failed. I tried to talk myself out of it: 'this only happens to old people,' and, 'only rich people lose everything.' I was neither, yet it was time to face up to it. Lyn had stood guarantor for my car and there was no way I was going to bring her down with me. Debbie had done a lot for me already, and I couldn't bear to ask for more help, or to tell Trevor, Mum and Dad what was really going on. Bills were overdue and debts were piling up. I didn't know how to fix the situation nor did I feel I had the strength. Analysing where and why it had gone wrong was not helping.

What did I want? I honestly did not know. I knew exactly what I did not want, but I didn't know what I actually wanted. In the short term though, cash was king, and that's where I focused.

I took on two more weekend jobs in addition to my current day job. I typed up examination papers for the school nearby. I took on the odd driving job – transporting people somewhere, anywhere in exchange for some cash. At the same time I took on an additional specialist study programme which I hoped would increase my chances of changing jobs and making more money to make ends meet. It was exhausting trying to fit it all in. The emotion was wearing me down too. I was giving life a lot, and didn't at all feel replenished in any way. The extra money got me through for another few months, but the debt lay untouched, and the rest of my life felt bleak. I knew the day would come when I would need to make another tough decision.

One night, as I wallowed in misery in the cold and the dark, I wrote out my vision for my life. After several iterations, I wrote, 'My vision for my life is to be free.' Underneath that I wrote down everything that freedom meant to me: free from the constraints of time, free to explore my mind, free from worry and anxiety, financial freedom, freedom to say and do what I want, and freedom to love and be loved. I stuck it inside my notebook to remind myself every day what I needed to be working towards. I needed a plan to make that vision a reality. Then I needed to find the strength and courage to execute that plan.

Shortly after defining my vision and the grand plan, the day arrived when it was time to leave that unhappy life behind. I was broken, exhausted and disillusioned, but the moment I made that decision to choose the life I wanted, nothing short of a series of miracles was set in motion. I miraculously got invited to interview with a major bank in another city. They flew me up for the interview – unheard of for a junior position. They offered me the job the next day. I needed to start a month later. In between, I randomly received a phone call from a letting agent, encouraging me to view a property which 'she heard'

(Goodness knows from whom!) I was looking for. It was perfect in every way, and I signed the lease agreement a few hours later.

I was excited and afraid at the same time. I still had to wrap up my 'old' life in Durban. Lyn was there every step of the way as the house got sold and debt repayment arrangements were put in place. I had to give away the bigger dogs – to this day that remains my deepest sadness. I was however able to keep my little white Maltese dog, Dusty, who was my anchor throughout those stormy seas and beyond.

When we finally packed up the house, Dusty and I set off on our 553km, 6h25 minute drive to our new home. Debbie helped Dusty and I settle into Johannesburg in the late 1990s.There was no looking back. Trevor made a trip from New York to make sure that I was okay. I kept reminding myself of my vision – to be free – and I always remember Mum and Dad drumming it into us that we were designed to be the best we can be, and only when this happened did I myself realise that I was not being my best before, that I needed to start believing in myself first before anyone else will.

That was a long time ago. Nowadays it is still that vision that I crafted on that bitterly cold night that drives me forward. When life knocks me over, my vision is what compels me to pick myself up. There were times when I didn't think it was possible to get back up again, until I came across Nick Vujicic, the Australian motivational speaker born with no limbs. In one of his videos he falls over and shows how he keeps trying to pick himself up without the benefit of having limbs. The image was so powerful. Eventually he does pick himself up. His words echo in my mind, '*If I fall, I will try 100 times to get up. If I fail, I will keep trying. If I give up, will I ever get up? No. Remember if you keep trying you will find a way eventually.*'

Truly inspirational. I pick myself up every time. And this is exactly what this chapter is about: Define your vision, keep moving forward, when you fall over, pick yourself up, keep moving, and eventually you will achieve your vision. Giving up or doing nothing, leaves you at the mercy of the circumstances around you.

Don't wait for calamity or catastrophe, heartbreak or bankruptcy before you define your vision. Do it now. Define your destiny. And if you're not sure how, then here are some tips.

How to define your vision

Envision a powerful life for yourself despite the environment you find yourself in, despite your circumstances, despite the challenges that lie ahead. You can no longer live by default: 'wait and see' is not an option any more. Focusing on your vision and developing an unwavering belief in your ability to take a step closer to it every day will ensure alignment between purpose and action. You cannot afford to follow a path that is not consistent with your ultimate life purpose, because a tough new world awaits your unique insight, and you cannot deny this period of ingenuity. You will have to tap into your heart and mind, be courageous in defining or uncovering that vision and moving forward toward it.

What is a personal vision and why have one?

Often when I ask my coaching clients what their vision for their lives is they are rarely able to define it. They tell me that they've never really thought about it. Eventually they come up with something that includes career, success and happiness with their families. They're not clear on how that breaks down into its component parts and, in trying to develop the vision bottom up, they're still unable to articulate what success means, how they'll know they have achieved it, how much money is enough and how it will be used.

Organisations are better at defining their visions. How else do they galvanise their employees to work toward a common task. Take Amazon and Apple, for example, as reported by *Forbes*:

Amazon: 'Our vision is to be earth's most customer centric company; to build a place where people can come to find and discover anything they might want to buy online.'

Apple (from an interview with CEO, Tim Cook): 'We believe that we are on the face of the earth to make great products and that's not changing. We are constantly focusing on innovating. We believe in the simple not the complex. We believe that we need to own and control the primary technologies behind the products that we make, and participate only in markets where we can make a significant contribution. We believe in saying no to thousands of projects, so that we can really focus on the few that are truly important and meaningful to us. We believe in deep collaboration and cross-pollination of our groups, which allow us to innovate in a way that others cannot. And frankly, we don't settle for anything less than excellence in every group in the company, and we have the self-honesty to admit when we're wrong and the courage to change. And I think regardless of who is in what job those values are so embedded in this company that Apple will do extremely well.'

Amazon's is short and to the point. Apple describes their value chain and, to an extent, includes aspects of their mission, i.e. the mechanisms by which the vision will be made a reality, for example, 'saying no to thousands of projects.'

As an individual, having a vision clarifies the direction in which to steer your life, it brings meaning to what you do, it helps to align your actions with your core values, and highlights your contribution to others. When living a life of purpose we feel 'in flow' and some of the greatest challenges seem effortless. Our sense of accomplishment is great because we worked toward something specific and we therefore appreciate it more once we've achieved it.

Tony Robbins during his 'Unleash the Power Within' seminars in London, described six basic human needs, which I believe come the closest to encapsulating what drives human behaviour:

- The need for certainty
- The need for variety
- The need for significance
- The need for love and connection
- The need for personal development
- The need for contribution

I believe a personal vision should comprise all these aspects for it to be truly fulfilling. Achieving your vision will bring stability, but must include variety to avoid boredom. Unless you yourself play a significant role in making your vision a reality it will not be fulfilling. Many people have inherited assets or reached the dizzy heights of fame and fortune, yet still feel unfulfilled. This is because one or more of the needs described above have not been met. Feeling connected to people around you makes for meaningful experiences, and you will need to feel that you have made a contribution to something bigger than yourself. You will need to gain some personal development from the experience too.

Your vision needs to speak to your passions, your dreams, your goals – as if time and money were no obstacle and failure not possible. Your vision needs to speak to who you are and the difference you want to make in the 'new' world. If you are thinking that you won't live that long so why bother, I would counter with there being no greater legacy than inspiring a generation of visionaries. It is more than just a fancy term – it is the indisputable part of who you are and how you will always be remembered.

> 'Success is not final, failure is not fatal:
> it is the courage to continue that counts,'
> WINSTON CHURCHILL (1874 – 1965)

So how do you define your vision?

If the word 'vision' feels too big or vague or unnatural to you, replace it with a term that you are comfortable with, e.g. my life plan, my life's worth, my journey or my purpose. Ensure that it is a big idea, not a little goal; a magnetic force not a minor task.

Whether you are one of those people who feel a sense of misalignment in themselves or have that feeling that something's missing, or perhaps you are just starting out and would like to know how, here are a few suggestions on how you can go about defining your vision:

- Create a vision statement – start by listing the words that move you, that speak to you on a profound level. Then craft a sentence of what you want to achieve for your life.
- Create a vision board – synthesise your vision into a visible collection of photos, pictures, drawings, artefacts of all the components of your vision. Include the words from your vision statement as well on your vision board.
- Create a vision scrapbook – it contains all the items of the vision board but is in album form.

Focus on bringing your vision to life. Describe your dream life as if you were living it already. Feel the excitement and the energy.

Whatever you come up with has to be enchanting. It needs to draw you in and propel you forward. It must be captivating and liberating all at once. In whatever format you choose to document it, keep it visible at the best times of day when you can focus on it.

A vision will always remain a fantasy unless you actively take steps to make it a reality.

- Now break down the vision you came up with above into 3-5 goals to be achieved over definite periods. Be clear on the dates.
- For each goal flesh out 5 to10 steps needed to achieve that goal.
- With each milestone you reach, remember to celebrate. You are living your dream, you deserve some acknowledgement!

What does it typically feel like to live your vision?

When interviewed as part of the research for this book, the faces of all the candidates who participated brightened, their postures grew and gestures became more animated as they excitedly described the feeling of 'being in flow'. I've summarised my favourite descriptions from them:

- ☺ You are following your intuition and it feels reasonably scary but exciting at the same time.
- ☺ You have 'that powerful feeling', that magnetic force that pulls you forward.
- ☺ You feel as if you are making a contribution to something bigger than yourself.
- ☺ Thoughts, words and actions 'flow' because they are aligned to your core values.

☺ You trust in an innate wisdom to get you through it, rather than focusing on what you don't have.

☺ You approach obstacles with a positive and empowering mind-set, e.g. 'I can handle it' or 'if it's meant to be then I will find a way'.

☺ If there was nothing else that you needed to do in life, this would be rewarding enough.

☺ You are fuelled with optimism to keep going even during times of adversity.

☺ Your sense of resolve grows steadfastly.

☺ You feel a sense of pride each time you've overcome an obstacle or achieved a milestone.

If you can relate to these feelings then, you are on the right track.

When is your vision not a true vision

When you are out of sync with your life purpose and vision, you feel:

☹ Like something is missing

☹ Disconnected somehow

☹ Frustrated and annoyed with little things

☹ Like life or everyday activities lack purpose

☹ Somewhat undervalued

☹ Dissatisfied about what you have

☹ Tired of working towards it

☹ Forced to do something against your will

☹ Like the voice inside is not your own but sounds more like a voice of authority (e.g. a parent, significant other, teacher) telling you what needs to be done

These thoughts and feelings are clues to misalignment. Deal with the feelings and emotions – they are nudging you to reconnect.

How will having a vision now benefit you in the new world?

In recent years we have become sceptics: doubtful that what we want will ever materialise despite our best efforts, and suspicious of 'the system' (whether the system is our parents, our school, our employers, the government, the rules of life, or even just our imposter syndrome – our negative self-talk). All this achieves is pessimism, which gnaws away at motivation and deteriorates into apathy and cynicism.

Focusing on the negative aspects of our lives preoccupies the brain; specifically, more neurons 'connect' to prepare for a fight or flight response. Adrenaline is triggered, resulting in physiological changes to the body such as an accelerated heart rate, blood flow shifting to the limbs and away from digestion. Prolonged stress and fear is detrimental to our health. We need to actively exercise the 'filters' in the brain that trigger responses appropriate to the situations we face. We need fresh thinking and a new way of living that addresses all of the challenges described in Chapter 1.

Whoever you are, whatever your lifestyle, background and education, your vision will galvanise you. It will move and inspire you to act; it will make you stand up and dust yourself off after you've fallen; and it will give you the oomph to keep going. It will bring out your boldness, it will shine through when you speak. That in itself will *inspire others to their greatness*, in the words of the great Marianne Williamson.

You will know it is the right vision because you will love it, you will feel strong emotion and passion around it. It will envelop you and energise you, not in spite of but because of your circumstances. You will live your purpose. So will people around you. Through the laws of nature, it will help you achieve harmony and balance. It will make for happier families, communities, workplaces, societies and eventually countries.

Get obsessed with and by your vision. Think about it. Often. Dedicate time every day to making progress toward it. Even if your vision is hazy, or unclear, step into the fog. Do not continue on the path of least resistance. Many clients operate on the 'if …then' principle: if they get more money then they can take time off to do the things they love, if they get that promotion then things will be easier. My advice is don't wait. Do it now. It may be that you start on a scale smaller than you had in mind. Just start now.

Live your vision. Become a visionary if you're that way inclined. Do things in unconventional ways if you need to. Visionaries are people who transform the landscape of our lives. They define the norms rather than conform to them. They do not make the most of them; they simply smash through them. They are the people who have many more failures under their belts, needing usually just one success to make it worthwhile. Thomas Edison is a prime example of this, 'failing' 10,000 times in developing the light bulb, but in sticking with his vision he transformed modern life as we know it, simply because he believed in it. The achievement of his vision set in motion a tidal wave of new beginnings on the horizon of life – building the infrastructure needed for a functioning bulb, providing electricity in homes and businesses, and completely powering up how we live, work and communicate.

They say hindsight has 20:20 vision, meaning that after the occurrence of an event, you can clearly see what could have been done better. I would like to change this saying to 'Mind-sight has 20:20 vision', where firm belief in investing the time needed to develop a vision for yourself now, will yield better results sooner.

Knowing what I know now, and if I had the chance to live my life over, would I? Absolutely! Would I change anything? Not a chance. Do I want more? Definitely!

Do you?

'The mind moves in the direction of
our currently dominant thoughts.'
EARL NIGHTINGALE (1921 – 1989).

THREE

ENQUIRING MINDS STRIVE FOR EXCELLENCE AND INNOVATION

'The important thing is not to stop questioning. Curiosity has its own reason for existing. One cannot help but be in awe when he contemplates the mysteries of eternity, of life, of the marvellous structure of reality. It is enough if one tries merely to comprehend a little of this mystery every day. Never lose a holy curiosity.'

ALBERT EINSTEIN (1879 – 1955)

Having gotten myself out of my pickle, I spent the next year in Johannesburg reflecting on my life, evaluating what was important to me, tracing back to where it started, and looking at the paths that lay ahead. There were 'duvet days' that kept me hidden from the world – exactly what I needed to repair the parts that I thought were broken. There were also some 'high energy days' where I needed to be outside exploring – and that was when Dusty and I would pack a picnic basket and go on one of our regular road-trips, heading out in different directions each weekend.

As I analysed the yin and yang in me, I realised that while tiredness and circumstances wore out my body, my enquiring mind was still thirsty for stimulation. It got me thinking about how to keep that enquiring mind alive even though circumstances around us may sap its strength. I had to find out where curiosity came from, and how to keep it alive.

Children!

I watched with intrigue as my 4- and 5-year old grandnieces Lea and Teeyana figured their way around an iPad, downloading just the free games that appealed to them, explaining to me that I was '*not allowed to download games that are outside my age range or which cost money, because Mum and Dad will be upset.*' I am impressed at how techno-savvy they are. Their dexterity is remarkable. They weren't taught how to use the devices, their mothers (my nieces) tell me. It was intuitive. So I ask Lea and Teeyana how they go about selecting the games and apps that they like and they explain, with some patience at my persistence in interrupting their playtime with such elementary questions, that it is because they are curious. The pictures look different and interesting, the colours are intriguing but pleasing on the eye, the screens are not too busy and not too empty – they tell me that some designers don't understand what makes them happy. And with each insight they impart I am more impressed than ever.

A few weeks later I am at a TEDx Conference in Johannesburg and one of the speakers showed how a 9-month old helps a 14-month old play a toddler's game on an iPad at their nursery school. I am in awe.

So began my journey of researching the enquiring mind and the power of curiosity. What better place to start than with Teeyana and Lea, and Lea's older brother Ethan (9). Claire (11) and Nicola (9), my youngest nieces, are also part of this conversation. Claire and Ethan smile at me sympathetically when I tell them that '*Back in my day we didn't have the internet …*' and I talk about the *Encyclopaedia Britannica* series that we used back then for research. Ethan asks, '*So did they become Wikipedia?*' and I of course fall off my chair at the missed opportunity that he was able to spot. As I continue to explain life in my day, it's clear that this is a world they can barely relate to.

Claire tells me, '*Children are born with curiosity but as they grow into adults they lose it, perhaps because they get too caught up in the busy-ness of life.*' So I ask them how to reignite that spark in adults, and their reply astonishes me: '*Grownups will only find the time and energy to be curious if it benefits them and the people they care about it, and if it makes them feel better, and usually that's all the same thing.*'

Were they right? Is it possible that while children are naturally inquisitive and will continue to be, adults who have 'lost it' can regain it if a need is met? I set out to test the theory.

It was very evident that people like Henry Ford all the way through to Bill Gates exhibited heightened interests in exploring the unknown. Their philosophy, it seemed, was this: just because it hasn't been done yet, doesn't mean it cannot be done. Henry Ford achieved this as he set out to develop unbreakable glass for windshields, something his most experienced engineers reported to be impossible to achieve at the time. Undeterred, Ford recruited a new team who, out of curiosity, came up with the formula for shatterproof glass. This fulfilled several 'needs' of his: the need to explore the unknown, the need to create something, the need to safeguard the lives of people who drove the cars he built.

Many of the world's greatest inventions were born the same way. If we believed the Commissioner at the US Patent Office in 1899 when he allegedly said, '*Everything that needs to be invented, already has been invented,*' where would we be today?

If people like Thomas Edison had lacked an enquiring mind, or gave up too easily, where would we be today? It got me thinking that if currently people are feeling too tired, uninspired or for whatever reason are failing to reignite that inquisitive mind, then we as a species are at risk of stagnating, and ultimately perishing. The rest of this chapter is dedicated to helping you develop an enquiring mind which strives for excellence and innovation, as this, I believe, is critical to shaping what we need in order to be ready for the new world.

The importance of cultivating an enquiring mind

Alice Munro, recipient of the Nobel Prize for Literature in 2013, summed it up beautifully when she said, *'The constant happiness is curiosity'*.

More than happiness, studies have shown that there is a positive correlation between intelligence and curiosity. The *Journal of Personality and Social Psychology* published a study in 2002, where researchers *'measured novelty-seeking behaviour in 1,795 3-year-olds, and then measured their cognitive ability at age 11. The 11-year-olds who had been highly curious 3-year-olds scored 12 points higher on total IQ compared with their low stimulation seeking counterparts. They were also reported to have superior scholastic and reading ability.'*

Other studies reveal that high curiosity levels in adults are linked to better problem-solving abilities and stronger analytical skills.

Sheena Iyengar, in her TED talk on the Art of Choosing, which is also the name of her book, describes the performance of children from various cultures on puzzles that they personally selected. She conducted an experiment with 7- to 9-year olds, which showed that Anglo-American children did twice as many anagram puzzles when they selected the puzzle themselves. However Asian-American children performed best when they believed their mothers chose; second best when they chose for themselves and least well when chosen by the facilitator, reinforcing the point that cultural norms have a huge influence on performance. Iyengar also says, *'When choice is thrust on people who are insufficiently prepared it no longer offers opportunities – instead it provides constraints. Choice is our ability to see and appreciate the differences between products and services. Too many choices make it overwhelming; it is not a matter of liberation but suffocation through minutiae.'* Seth Godin, author, speaker, entrepreneur, supports this idea, and says if we have too much choice in an era where we have too little time, then we tend to ignore the choices.

Ignoring choices means living by default.

How do we reignite it? If Meg Jay in her TED Talk is right, that our twenties is a critical time in adult development, then are we entering that decade in the right frame of mind, and for the older generation, are we interacting with that generation appropriately? Jay, a clinical psychologist who specialises in twenty-somethings, says that her studies have shown that the brain 'rewires' itself for adulthood in our twenties, that the first 10 years of our careers determines our earning potential and that 80% of life's defining moments happen by age 35. If this is the case then we must not trivialise the importance of this period of our lives.

For me curiosity is not a badge that one acquires at a point in life. It needs to be nurtured from now, irrespective of one's age. In order to develop the solutions for the future, *'There will be a greater need to embark on the path of life with a renewed sense of wonder and doubt,'* as Jim Canterucci, author of *Personal Brilliance*, aptly describes it. *'Curiosity is about actively exploring the environment, asking challenging questions, investigating possibilities for innovation.'* He says you *learn more* because you want to *know more.*

How to develop an enquiring mind

By exploring new concepts and ideas, undertaking research, exercising critical thinking and analytical skills, one enhances one's intelligence. *'Study hard what interests you the most in the most undisciplined, irreverent and original manner possible,'* said Richard Feynman, one of the world's best known scientists. Deeper levels of knowing strengthen how you relate to others, develop stronger social relationships and therefore enable you to bring the best out in people.

An enquiring mind has positive health implications for older people too. In a 1996 study published in *Psychology and Aging*, more than 1,000 adults aged between 60 and 86 were observed over a five-year period. '*Researchers found that those who were more curious at the beginning of the study were more likely to be alive at its conclusion, even after taking into account age, whether they smoked, the presence of cancer or cardiovascular disease, and so on. It is possible that declining curiosity is an initial sign of neurological illness and declining health. Nonetheless, there are promising signs that enhancing curiosity reduces the risk for these diseases and may even reverse some of the natural degeneration that occurs in older adults.*'

In my youth, learning was the ability to memorise content en-masse, and regurgitate as much of it as possible against the appropriate question during an exam. My skills at this earned me good marks! As I got older I began questioning the application of what I had learned, but only the best amongst my teachers could help me relate it to the real world. Even though I received an A-grade in mathematics in my final year of high school, I have yet to figure out how to apply trigonometry to my life – sin, cos and tan are high on my bucket list!

The love of learning must become a lifestyle choice in adulthood, and as adults we need to keep it alive in children. The more we demonstrate inquisitiveness, the more open we become, we meet more people, and collaborate with them to create solutions and things far greater than ourselves – the proverbial sum of all parts is greater than the whole. Children observe this in us and copy what they see.

In his book, *The Power of Premonitions* (2009), Larry Dossey MD, cites studies that have shown '*Women who regularly engage in mini-mysteries… taking on novel experiences that get them out of familiar routines (better) preserve their mental faculties later in life.*' In short, a regular dose of the unexpected helps keep your brain healthy. A 2005 report in the journal *Health Psychology*, described a two-year study involving more than 1,000 patients. '*It found higher levels of curiosity were also associated with a decreased likelihood of developing hypertension and diabetes. While correlation does not imply causation, these relationships suggest that curiosity may have a variety of positive health benefits that will require further investigation in future.'*

Many schools in the UK and the US adopt enquiry-based teaching approaches from as early as age eight, as a means of preparing children for the future I described in Chapter 1. An enquiry-based (as opposed to 'transmission-based') learning programme's objectives are set, and the class teacher is tasked with ensuring they are met, however the class is largely self-driven, in that students focus on an area of interest to them whilst still developing skills. It is a significant step away from the traditional teacher-at-centre learning environment where the teacher teaches skills and content, to a more collaborative student-led enquiry based learning methodology. It is also a way of making learning more relevant to students' lives and sees children taking increasing responsibility for determining the content and purpose of their learning. While extensively applied in developed countries such as the UK, North America, Australasia, parts of Europe and Asia, the use of a variety of media to enhance the learning experience continues to grow in developing countries like South Africa, and other African and South American countries.

Integrating an enquiry-led approach into a standard curriculum will be powerful in developing the right balance of cognitive ability with content knowledge needed for the future.

The only challenge is the time it may take for these governments to realise the criticality of creating this type of learning environment, and mobilise the resources to deliver this effectively. I discuss this in more detail in Chapter Five, but waiting for this transformation in education to happen is not an option, I am afraid. So if you have children, it is time for you to create an enquiry-based learning environment in your home. If you don't have children, the techniques provided later in this chapter describe equally how to stimulate creativity in adults.

Lifelong learning begins when life begins. Some parents, however, miss opportunities to develop their children's cognitive abilities at crucial stages in the child's life. In a world where information is readily available, ignorance is no longer an acceptable excuse. Redefine the role of a tiger mum or dad – be ferocious in developing curiosity, not in controlling them to succeed.

'*Curiosity dimmed is a future denied*', says Bruce Duncan Perry, author of *Curiosity: The Fuel for Development.* Perry says that our potential, the collection of emotional, social, and cognitive abilities, is expressed through the quantity and quality of our experiences. The less-curious child is less sociable, less knowledgeable and less active. They are harder to teach because they are harder to engage. Three of the key reasons as to why this might be the case are down to what adults do that impedes the naturally curious child. They impose their own fears on the child, reducing the child's natural willingness to explore; their disapproval of a child's actions curtails the child's enthusiasm; and finally parents who are not present, either physically or emotionally to celebrate a discovery or good deed inhibit the development of the child.

Here are some simple techniques to help develop an enquiring mind in children.

Tell children stories – this can be started from birth. If you can't afford a book or a library is not in close proximity, make up stories. Get creative. Get children used to listening, imagining and concentrating from an early age.

Engage children in the stories you tell – point out the shapes and the colours and then get them to mimic you. Change the tone of your voice for each character in the story and, again, get them to try to copy the sound you make. Make the story sound exciting. Capture the magic of stories through your voice, your choice of words, your actions. Make it fun. This can be started with children from as young as 4-months old. If you don't have a book, use objects around you, draw pictures – even in sand.

Provide your children with toys and games to stimulate brain interaction. The sense of touch when added to visual and audio stimuli makes for a heightened brain experience. Toys are not always available I fully appreciate, but children can get very creative with the environment – sand, stones, leaves, sticks and branches can become useful props, if needed.

When they get to the crawling stage, encourage children to explore their natural environments and be adventurous. Use encouraging words and a gentle tone of voice. Obviously, point out the dangers with a firmer tone!

As children get older, asking questions which require them to explain their understanding, feelings and experiences to you exercises the synaptic connections in their brain. Continual exercising of these synapses strengthens the assimilation of learning, improving the speed at which information is absorbed, processed and recalled.

Ignore tantrums and encourage desired behaviour. Do not reward good behaviour with food, gifts or treats. Behaviour scoring charts are powerful mechanisms to drive the required behaviours, and are best done in conjunction with the child. Good behaviour results in additional 'stars' being awarded and placed on the chart for visual impact. Undesirable behaviour is approached with disappointment and seriousness, but also in a somewhat conciliatory tone which encourages the desired behaviour. This is again done in conjunction with the child. When they've earned an agreed number of stars, it converts to a treat or a gift, which is somewhat of a mini-vision: something that the child is working towards.

Get them to link concepts, characters and stories. This expands thinking, reasoning and learning by association which in turn builds capacity to process complex situations in the brain for later in life.

Health warning – please apply age-appropriate challenge and support – too much or too little of each could be demotivating or may cause your child to lose interest.

HOW TO DEVELOP AN ENQUIRING MIND IN YOUNG CHILDREN (UP TO 9 YEARS OLD)

I realise in today's busy world, dedicating significant amounts of time to young children at regular times of day on an individual basis can be difficult. I also appreciate that even when time permits, children's responses to our questions go along the lines of, "Okay", "Nothing", "Don't know", and "Can't remember".

Here are some tips on how to get them engaged and how to develop an enquiring mind in older children.

Mix up the style of questions you ask the child. Even though I am sure you make use of open questions, make them intriguing. Infuse your questions with engaging comments. Change the tonality of your voice. Sound playful. Make it enticing. You could start questions off with: *'I wonder how …' 'I wish I knew …', 'What do you think would happen if … ?'* These types of questions engage the brain in a different way. They add emotion and purpose to the question being asked, making for a more rewarding experience for the child in finding the answers.

Show attentiveness when listening to the answers from children. Active listening such as nodding and smiling show that you are considering their response and encourages the child to continue. Do not interrupt them or correct their language or grammar as they speak. It damages confidence and removes the diligence if they feel that questions and answers simply result in criticism. Do not straighten their clothing or hair. Stay completely focused.

Be aware of your facial expressions as you listen to them, whilst considering their responses as well as when you reply. Children can be discouraged by a scowl or a frown even if it was not intended.

When responding to their answers, start off with the positives – comment on what points were well made, what you agree with, what you have learnt from it. Engage with them in an encouraging tone. Do not ruin the experience by adding a 'but' or a 'however' to the conversation at any time. It creates a conditioned response in children (and adults) knowing that a 'but' is coming, so they neglect to listen or forget the positive comments that were made.

Ask questions at the end. Do so in a kind way, with a gentle tone and a curious almost playful manner. Do not ask questions in a way that makes them feel that you don't believe them or that you are interrogating them, or looking to find fault.

Start by introducing one challenging question at a time. Then ask two or three. Keep your tone neutral. This will help build resilience in your children. It will enable them to think on their feet, maintain a level head under pressure, and remain focused on providing a good answer to a tough question. It builds confidence.

HOW TO DEVELOP AN ENQUIRING MIND IN OLDER CHILDREN (10+ YEARS OLD)

The next stage in continuing the development of an enquiring mind in older children is to observe where the child's interests lie and encourage and support them to take a deeper interest in it. Approach this with 'fascination at their fascination' in areas of interest. Support their interest by creating an environment in which this interest can be explored further, whether it's an information-oriented interest, a sport or a hobby like playing a musical instrument. Provide an environment where exposure to like-minded people is made possible. Whatever the subject, it must be of interest to the child, they must have initiated wanting to investigate it further, and it must have meaning for the child. Whatever the subject or project, it must be of interest to the child, they must have initiated wanting to investigate it further, and it must have meaning for the child.

As they embark on this journey, play the role of 'coach'. You learn with them, alongside them. You role model the curiosity you want to inspire in them. Ask them questions that get them to critically analyse, think and engage with the area of interest in a creative way. Explore their willingness to draw on a variety of related subjects to enhance learning. Travel, maps and geography can be extremely exciting for children, as can science, maths, music and art if used correctly. At the appropriate time, encourage them to add some challenge to their project. This exercises the brain, increases analytical abilities and enhances memory and recollection. Showing your interest by asking them questions that appeal to both logical reasoning and feelings is important. Remember also to encourage involvement of the five senses. Pedagogically after two weeks of learning, according to Edgar Dale's Cone of Learning Model, we retain 10% of what we read, 20% of what we see, 30% of what we hear, 50% of what we see and hear, 70% of what we say, and up to 90% of what we say and do.

Promote group working. It is important to recognise all contributions and to balance the reward for all participants. Encourage them to seek the opinions of others – exposure to feedback early on builds resilience, and promotes the desire to achieve self-mastery later in life. A bit of competition might be healthy between teams; it teaches one of life's greatest lessons that winning is not everything. Too much emphasis on winning ruins the social dynamic and the experience of working together. Focusing on outcomes and balancing with relationship dynamics is an important consideration. Learning how to articulate it will build confidence.

Assist the child to provide a balanced report on findings. Help the child on how to structure their thoughts and how to deliver concise accounts of findings. Inevitably they will come up with unique insights, which will be hugely empowering for them.

As their coach, each of the techniques above are characterised with questions.

Questions prompt further thought, analysis, discussion and debate. Provide balanced and constructive feedback with the primary objective being to develop confidence. That being said, it is important however, to make it fun and interesting always. Instant gratification will ensure repeat behaviour, repeat behaviour results in habits, and good habits are a great thing.

In order for these approaches to be effective, I believe there needs to be a cascade effect from adult to child. Adults need to model the curiosity to inspire children. And for those adults who don't have children, you are not off the hook! You need to be a role model to other adults too!

HOW TO DEVELOP AN ENQUIRING MIND IN ADULTS

Why bother, I hear some of you ask. It's too late... I can't make a difference... my time is done... I hear these cries of woe all too often. It keeps us stuck. *'Procrastination is the thief of time,'* Dickens said.

Don't just dip a toe in, jump right in, and as I know that is easier said than done, here are some techniques to inspire an enquiring mind in yourself and in other adults too.

Look at the areas in your life that matter to you. For example you may be contemplating a change in career, starting a business, or taking up a new hobby. It might also be that someone close to you needs some help.

If you are lacking drive, start by simply daydreaming about the end state. Forget about how you are going to get there, just enjoy being, living and feeling the end state. Visualise it, draw it, or write it out. Be clear on what good looks. Play with the idea of when you would like to see that situation materialise – set a date.

Ask yourself why this is important to you. This is crucial to fuelling your actions. If your 'why' is not big enough or important enough, then procrastination sets in. Ask yourself the following questions: Why do you need to do this? Why now? What will happen if you don't take action?

Then start by asking yourself questions like 'What's the first step I need take to take to move closer to this goal? What can I do today? What resources do I need?

Always approach it with an attitude of playfulness. If it feels like fun it will get done, if it feels like a chore then you are doing something wrong. Start over. Neuro-linguistic programming suggests that you reframe situations that you are not keen on in a more positive way, and change your association to it which will then give you the impetus to take action.

Similarly if a thought or idea is sparked, act on it immediately. I believe life is all about synchronicity, and doing things at the appropriate time helps with the flow. Find out more about your thought or idea. Do some research. Talk to some people. Feel excited.

Convince yourself that uncertainty and ambiguity is a good thing. If you are looking into something new, it may feel uncomfortable. That's all right. Stay with it. It's a good thing. Believe that there is pleasure in surprise. The joy in discovering new things is wonderful. Look forward to that until the discomfort passes.

These tips and techniques are designed to stimulate a drive in both adults and children alike that propels you forward, that makes you want to try, to keep going even when the chips are down. I believe it eliminates complacency, it removes the acceptance of mediocrity and annihilates debilitating feelings of defeat. It does however need continuous reinforcement. And repetition. And you will have then developed the best generation for the future.

Be the best you can be. Model the curiosity you want to inspire in others.

Why is it important to develop now for the future

Curiosity is like a magnet. It ignites in others the pursuit of happiness and draws like-minded people on the same quest as you, to you. Teamwork makes for better solutions, delivered faster and with greater impact. Creating an active mind that is solution-oriented, results in better quality decision-making and superior thought processes.

Enquiring minds will birth innovative solutions for advancements in space colonisation, energy and food production for our future. Demonstrating a mind-set of openness and positivity from now creates greater agility and responsiveness to problems and issues. Curiosity means a willingness to search for and consider more information, and therefore brings a better perspective. One is able to take a balanced view on the facts based on solid reasoning and measured responses; this brings objectivity to what you do.

Mastering the development of an enquiring mind places us at the start line of the race to save our species before it is too late. Are you in the starting line-up? Or are you a spectator in the race of life?

Curiosity is fuel for the brain. Fill up now.

My vision ignited my curiosity to get out of the stands and get into the race. My curiosity opened up lanes to worlds I hadn't even dreamt about.

Two years after packing it all in and moving to Johannesburg with Dusty, I started a new life in the world of management consulting. It took me on what can only be compared to a Steven Spielberg type movie – thrilling, adventurous, fast-paced – but it was real and it was my life! I could not have imagined such a fulfilling life, despite the ups and downs. Dusty and I moved to London – the poor boy endured six months of quarantine for me, but after that we were just fine. I was in my mid-twenties then, working for a major consulting firm, and ironically ended up specialising in organisational change, improving business performance and eventually coaching people on their own personal transformation journeys, helping them achieve phenomenal results for their lives. I guess I shouldn't have been surprised – my life experience was perfect training ground for this.

Every new client and organisation brought with it experiences that were rewarding beyond belief. I travelled a lot – every new city was culturally rich and breath-taking. I was curious so I said 'yes' to everything and the world around me just seemed to open up, and offered so many enriching experiences.

Over the years I met and worked with incredibly talented and kind people. I made some amazing new friends and made a difference to people's lives. It humbled me. Dusty passed on, I fell in love again, and Shakeer, Jazzy and Lucy became my London family (Jazzy and Lucy are Shih-Tzus, for the avoidance of doubt, with loads of personality). My world felt meaningful again. I learnt so much from life about life and, most importantly, I got to share it with so many people around the world. I couldn't be more blessed. My vision pointed me in the direction of self-discovery, and curiosity awakened my zest for life. All I had to do was say 'yes' to everything. How else could I be free?

And I was truly free for many years, or so I thought, blissfully unaware that something was changing without me noticing. And then on one fateful day, it happened. My life changed overnight.

I can't quite work out whether the change was afoot for 18 months, or 24 hours, or just in that moment when I reached for that cup, but it was all change from there.

FOUR

ENTERPRISING BEHAVIOURS THAT ACCELERATE ENTREPRENEURIAL INNOVATION

'The telephone has too many shortcomings
to be a means of communication.'
EXECUTIVE, WORLD'S LEADING TELEGRAPH COMPANY, 1876

'I think there is a world market for maybe five computers.'
CHAIRMAN IBM, 1943

'Guitar music is on the way out.'
RECORDING EXECUTIVE WHO REJECTED THE BEATLES, 1962

They said he 'lacked talent and imagination
and would amount to nothing.'
THEY WERE TALKING ABOUT MR WALT DISNEY.

If we focused on failure and didn't persevere, we wouldn't be where we are today. If we accepted the perspectives from the so-called authorities of the world, we will have been denied a world of richness. Be a disrupter, be an entrepreneur, be a positive force in the face of adversity.

There are numerous resources out there to help you embark on the path of an entrepreneur, but this is not what this chapter is about. What this chapter focuses on instead are the enterprising qualities of entrepreneurs who mostly started with nothing more than an idea, and converted it into one or more multi-million dollar businesses: Apple, Google, Boeing, Ford, Amazon, GE and Disney are all examples of companies started by entrepreneurial thinking. They are the 'pure' examples. The other alternative to achieving success is to contribute to the ecosystem that surrounds an entrepreneurial wave or a new invention. For example: accessories for Apple products are produced by many suppliers who enjoy huge returns on the back of Apple's success.

The entrepreneurs who birthed these business successes were clearly children with a sense of curiosity. *Forbes* reported that the 39 youngest people on the 2014 Billionaires list have a combined net worth of $115.7 billion. I was intrigued to know what common attributes they possessed to yield such incredible results. Where did the audacity of hope and courage come from? Could it be replicated? Moreover, I was fascinated at how, despite abject failures, bankruptcy and other cataclysmic disasters, they bounced back almost renewed in strength, confidence and determination, time and time again.

My first instinct was, 'I want to be that when I grow up!' Then I remembered, I am already all grown up! 'And by the way, didn't you lose everything once? Wanna do that again for fun now, do you?' said that taunting, impostor voice in my head. And with that I shut the lid on the thought. Curiosity, however, got the better of me again (I know now why they say curiosity killed the cat). Yes, I considered myself smart and successful; working for top management consultancy firms did a lot to build my confidence. Yes, I had been virtually bankrupt once, and I definitely did not want to go there again, but I was intrigued by the way entrepreneurs dealt with their challenges compared to the way I had handled mine back then. It bothered me that I hadn't handled my failures as well as they did. My lack of courage bothered me. There was also a restlessness in me about something I couldn't quite put my finger on. My body ached. I was denying something. There I was, earning a safe, regular salary from a regular job, yet I lived in fear of losing it all (again) one day. But here *they* were, willingly taking risks, merrily subjecting themselves to the instability of the open market, losing everything, making it all up again, year after year. How on earth?

I needed to know how this was done. I knew that if I could understand it and the psychology behind it, I would be a better person for it. I could also share it with more people, and inspire more people to tap into and develop their enterprising capabilities.

I racked my brain to work out how to understand this better. How do I research it? How will I convey the somewhat bleak message of an exponential growth in population with associated environmental and business challenges whilst still inspiring people to feel good about the advantages of fewer jobs and less remuneration? How could I legitimately coach or provide consulting advice to business owners on how to turn their businesses around and more importantly how to develop a mind of steel to thrive in adversity, without having experienced it myself?

I read books, I did research and I spoke to lots of people. I started going to seminars. There seemed to be over a dozen millionaires coming to South Africa to host seminars about 'how to become a millionaire,' and while many people got value from those seminars, I didn't. I just wanted to figure out the mind of the millionaire, not buy their products. I needed a different angle.

The answer hit me hard. I was shocked at the realisation. I called Alison, my best friend, immediately. She is my voice of reason. She asked me some tough questions. By the end of the call it was as clear as day – I needed to quit my six-figure senior role with a top consultancy firm in London and go solo.

On some level there was something bothering me about all this:

why was I entertaining the idea of leaving corporate to venture into the unknown? What was I unhappy about that was drawing me away from my life as it was? What was I sensing about the life of an entrepreneur that was appealing? What was going on with me? When did it change for me? Was it that fateful day when I reached for a cup, or was it that horrid night at Tottenham Court Road Station, or perhaps it started from way before that? Do I really go solo now?

I did. It took a day for the shock to subside. Two weeks elapsed from realisation to resignation from my company – in between came Christmas, New Year, and the twist: I decided to move back to South Africa to start this new venture. I called a family meeting – Shakeer was keen, and arranging a transfer with his company was possible, while Jazzy and Lucy did not object to more sunshine. Done deal. The added complication of not having lived or worked in South Africa in over 12 years was that I had lost my personal and professional networks, so I was starting a business with no client base, and nowhere to live and work when we got there.

So we did the next best thing. We bought a house off the internet, without me seeing it. I had lost my mind, but that's okay, I remember thinking at the time, I will find it later. The other thing I knew I had to change to make this a success was to adopt a different mind-set. So I pretended that I was 'retiring to the sun' and, like some people take up a new hobby in their retirement, I decided to start my own consulting and coaching business. To make it a bit interesting, I gave myself exactly two years to get from idea to a profitable business with several income generating streams tagged to it. A two-year long income-generating retirement! Not a bad idea, albeit a somewhat mad idea. After that I would decide where to next.

Ten weeks and 34 miracles later, furniture from a 3-storey house and two cars left Southampton Port in two containers on a ship, while two dogs and two humans flew out of Heathrow airport at minus 4°C, landing in Johannesburg's O.R. Tambo airport at 29°C with only one certainty – it was going to be sunny for the majority of the year!

Leaving the airport, I felt as if I had forgotten something. There's always that one thing. What was it? Dogs, check; bags, check; phone, check; wallet, check. My whole family were at Debbie's house in Johannesburg awaiting our arrival. They were expecting us for dinner. We always made a trip at that time of year, every year. Ah, then I remembered. Although I'd been in contact with them, and told them about the packing, I had neglected to mention that packing meant packing up the whole house, not just suitcases, and that we'd actually moved back. I guess arriving with the dogs in tow was a dead giveaway!

They did well to mask the surprise. After five whole seconds their curiosity turned to concern. Retirement, reserved for either the old or the young rich, which I was neither, left them questioning my sanity. I couldn't bring any money into the country, the move had cost us a fortune, living life to the full meant that I had no savings, I wanted to start a business in between soaking up some much needed sunshine, I was only 38-years old and I wanted to call *that* retirement? How is that retirement, they asked.

'Well, I don't want to wait my whole life for the end of my life to be the best part of my life experienced at the worst time of my life. So I'm doing it now,' I replied.

Besides, with the hours I'd clocked up working over the years, I was more like 57 years old, so it shouldn't be too much of a stretch to consider that I was on early retirement! Retired people do things they love. I wanted exactly that. Whether it was taking up a new hobby, or following an existing one more diligently, taking up a sport, going travelling or doing some gardening, I wanted the same. I wanted to do something I love in retirement; the only difference is I wanted retirement to start now.

I also wanted to make a difference in the world and the bills still needed to be paid, so starting my own business made sense – consulting for organisations on strategy and transformation, as well as coaching people on how to achieve personal excellence in their lives. So far my business is going exceptionally well, with lots of highs and some lows, but as I am learning, I am making a difference and that is all that matters.

Half expecting me to go back to England after a few months, my family eventually came around. It is great being back. The transition was tough. Not everyone enjoys coming back, and many people want to leave the country. I believe it was the spirit of an enterprising mind-set that got me into a good space. The rest of this chapter is dedicated to helping you develop a mind-set that works for you by drawing on the experiences of the entrepreneurial greats of all time.

What will it take for you to 'start your retirement' now?

Researching the enterprising behaviours exhibited by entrepreneurs

I mentioned earlier that I have researched some of the world's greatest entrepreneurs, business leaders, sports and entertainment icons, and read as much of their printed work as possible. People like Richard Branson, Steve Jobs, Bill Gates, Mark Zuckerberg, Donald Trump, Warren Buffett, Oprah Winfrey, Stephen Covey, Jack Welch, Madonna, Lady Gaga, Tiger Woods, David Beckham and others bring such interesting perspectives on how they made their fortunes. It is safe to say that they all had a vision, they all had enquiring minds and they all displayed enterprising qualities to have reached such notoriety in short timescales.

Who would have guessed a poor little girl, born in Mississippi and raised in Milwaukee by a single teenage mother, raped at nine years of age, giving birth aged 14 to a son who died shortly thereafter, would have grown into a megastar? Meet Oprah Winfrey. Oprah started her career in radio whilst still in high-school. She then moved into the evening news and eventually day-time TV. The Oprah Winfrey show was the highest-rated talk show in TV history, and has won her several awards. She's also an amazing philanthropist who donates a cut of her $1.3 billion net worth to a variety of causes benefitting women, children and families.

Richard Branson, when interviewed by *Entrepreneur Magazine*, described the five 'secrets' to business success. He came up with these reflections on what characterised Virgin's many ventures and what went wrong when they didn't get it right.

- Enjoy what you are doing – for the effort and time and to make enough to pay the bills, love what you do.
- Create something that stands out – look at what the most successful businesses have done (then look at what the competition is doing, provide what's missing, and close the gap).
- Create something that everybody who works for you is really proud of (Branson puts employees first, customers second and shareholders third).
- Be a great leader.
- Be visible (where it matters).

RICHARD BRANSON

One of my favourite quotes from Richard Branson, published by *Business Pundit*, is:

> 'The thing to learn from history is that the best never, never, never disappear. The best clubs are still here 21 years later, the best hotels, the best airlines, and so it is actually worthwhile not listening to the accountants sometimes. I mean accountants forever have said, you know, if you'd take out the bar in your plane you can put another six seats in... '

Both Madonna and Lady Gaga are good examples of disrupters to the status quo. According to the *Guinness Book of World Records*, Madonna *'boasts a net worth of over $400 million on the strength of 200+ million album sales around the world.'* Lady Gaga, also a good example of success, takes an uncommon approach to her music. She made it big because of being controversial, exhibiting non-conformity, and expressing herself freely. People relate to her because she very possibly represents their best ideas of themselves; that's why I believe she is popular.

After months of research, which I have applied to my personal circumstances, tested and refined at length, I have distilled what I believe to be the 10 Enterprising Behaviours needed for the future.

DEFINE A COMPELLING REASON FOR DOING WHAT YOU DO

Every successful person that I researched was motivated toward achieving a goal. Sometimes it's a negative experience that repositioned the direction in which they faced, but ultimately they had a reason for why they wanted to achieve a goal. Why do you want to be a success in this world? Why now? What will happen if you do not follow your goal? Having a solid reason that drives you forward means that nothing that anybody says, whether it is criticism, ridicule or blame, will stop you from progressing. No circumstance or calamity will hold you back. You will not be distracted or disillusioned, and disappointment will act only as fuel to spur you on. It doesn't matter to you whether it has not been done before or whether previous attempts have failed. You are motivated beyond reason to find a way to make your dream a reality. Remember your reason is not about what you no longer want. It is about what you want. And your reason needs to be compelling enough to prompt you to take action. So find your reason now.

ADOPT A MIND-SET OF READINESS TO TAKE ON ANY CHALLENGE

No one can truly be ready for everything, and it would be stupid to try, but adopting a mind-set of readiness to take on any challenge that presents itself is what makes the difference between success and failure. Whether it's readiness to cope, readiness to change tactics, or readiness to try something new, are you ready for whatever comes your way? Underpinning readiness, is simply trusting that you will be able to cope with anything that comes your way, that you will make the most of any situation. It's not about blind faith, it's about gearing up for what you are going after.

'If you choose to not deal with an issue, then you give up your right of control over the issue and it will select the path of least resistance.'
SUSAN DEL GATTO (2009)

ADOPT A MIND-SET OF RESOURCEFULNESS

No one person will have all the skills, knowledge or behavioural attributes to make a business successful. However, believing in your ability to find the required resources and trusting your instinct to apply the right level of resources at the appropriate times is the key to longevity. Knowing when to inject creativity, acting on ideas quickly, and exploiting opportunities at the right time will enable you to gain competitive advantage. Resourcefulness requires that you take initiative; that you recognise your weaknesses and celebrate your strengths; that you have the courage to admit this to yourself and engage the right people in their areas of specialism.

'A year from now you may wish you had started today.'
KAREN LAMB (2013)

ADOPT A MIND-SET OF NO REGRET

Trusting that you did the best you could at the time with the resources that you had available requires true strength of character. Believing that there is no failure only learning can be hugely empowering. This is a conscious choice you need to make and takes time to create. One of the best ways of eliminating the risk of regret, is to simply start immediately. There are many evils that hold us back. Procrastination is the most popular. Dive in. Headlong. Any mistakes, will therefore become learning opportunities. A relative of procrastination is known as perfectionism – the tendency to wait until everything is perfect before you can dive in. It does not serve you. There is no right time for anything. Just doing the best you can is all that is necessary.

Low self-belief is another evil that cripples the spirit, if you let it. It is your life. Take charge now.

'The pessimist sees difficulty in every opportunity; the optimist sees opportunity in every difficulty,'
WINSTON CHURCHILL (1874 – 1965)

REFRAME YOUR SITUATION IN A POSITIVE WAY

This can be one of the most difficult things to do when you are in the middle of a crisis. The urgency of needing to resolve the issue and the heightened emotions cause a brain-drain, and you are at risk of making a knee-jerk decision and regretting it later. Instead, reframing the situation in a different way may give you an alternative perspective from which to act.

Change positions. Place yourself in the shoes of the other person. Force yourself to see the positives in a bad situation, find higher meaning in the experience. This will take some time as you work through the emotion that clouds your better judgement. It may help you to participate in a role play with a friend Or, if you have one, to work through with your coach. In time you will see the value gained, although it might be difficult for you to admit at first. See challenges as opportunities to be better, regard the pitfalls as springboards to achieve greater heights, consider the forks in the road as paths to diversify, and be grateful for life showing you something you would otherwise have missed or avoided.

DEVELOP A HIGH TOLERANCE FOR RISK

This requires you to take the necessary steps to learn how to assess and manage risk. Developing a high tolerance for risk is not an excuse for recklessness. Decisions made from anxiety are not solutions to managing risk. Developing a high tolerance for risk will enable you to stretch your boundaries and gain exposure to new situations. It works hand in hand with resourcefulness – knowing who to pull in and when to back out. Risk is about keeping a watchful eye, analysing the trends, taking advantage of calculated opportunities, but ultimately going with your gut. It's about having faith and patience, sounding out people's opinions but ultimately following *informed* instincts.

Many people set out on their life journeys chasing money. Money is the vision, the goal and the measure of success all in one. Once they have it they don't know what to do with it. It gets squandered. It becomes unappreciated. It breeds discontent. It finances destructive behaviour to compensate for feelings of low self-esteem. It cripples the potential for success.

What determines whether money 'sticks' or not is your money threshold. T. Harv Ecker calls the beliefs that drive your relationship with money your 'money blueprint'. Have you defined how much money you would like to have? Have you thought about what you would do with it if you had it? Have you thought about how you would save or invest it? Saving is one thing, hoarding is another. Have you ever wondered why lottery winners lose their money so quickly yet self-made millionaires can make it back again relatively quickly? Are your beliefs and behaviours driving you to be a money magnet?

Examine your beliefs about money. Define a figure in monetary terms that you would like to make and specify the date by which you would like to achieve it. How does the figure make you feel? Does it scare you or excite you? If it scares you too much the likelihood is that you will not achieve it. Therefore you need to lower the number so that it is meaningful, exciting but also a bit of a stretch. How realistic is the time-frame? If the balance of excitement with a little bit of fear pushes you to achieve the financial goal, that's a good thing, but if the timings overwhelm or paralyse you, re-examine them.

Next, break down the figure into achievable increments or milestones. For example, if the goal is to make £1.2 million in 12 months' time, then you need to work out whether that breaks down into making £100,000 per month, or £250,000 in your first quarter, £800,000 by the third quarter and so on. Now perform a gap analysis against your milestone plan. If the goal is to make £100,000 per month starting from your first month, but you're only making £15,000 per month, then there is a significant gap to fill. Two things need to happen: reality check and brainstorm. Are you being realistic with how to close the gap between £15,000 and £100,000 in 30 days? What is the master plan that is going to get you there? £100,000 may well be achievable, but is month one realistic?

The Secret by Rhonda Byrne is a great book, which speaks of the 'Law of Attraction'. And yes indeed, the Universe provides. However, using Newton's First Law of Motion developed in the 1600s, where an object will remain in a state of inertia unless acted upon by a force, you therefore must take action for something to materialise. Bear in mind the wise words of the great Einstein, *'We can't solve problems by using the same kind of thinking we used when we created them.'* So brainstorm what you need to do to achieve the larger sums of money. Take action every day.

RESILIENCE IS INTRINSIC STRENGTH

There is plenty of academic research on different aspects of resilience. Learning how to cope with the knocks, bounce back, and persevere through trying times will enable you to stay on course, they say. Building a support network of like-minded people around you is one way to do this; whether you are a parent having a difficult time with your children or a new entrepreneur adapting to the ebbs and flows of business, having other people around you to share experiences with and lessons learned, is incredibly useful.

I have, though, a different view about resilience and what is needed for the future. I believe that we are all intrinsically resilient. We all have the mental strength, stamina, perseverance and ability to operate from a peak state of mind. I believe that sometimes we lose focus, concentration or self-belief and the force field is temporarily weakened. We opt out. I believe that you would have very different results if you believed resilience to be your natural state – reacquiring it simply becomes a decision. It is not a muscle that you have to build with repeated behaviour.

So try it. Think about an unpleasant situation in your life that knocked you off course. Consider how you would have preferred to handle it. What prevented you from bouncing back? What was missing? Stand up for a moment as you read this. Take a walk around the room or the area you are in to get your heart rate up a little and to improve circulation. Increased oxygen to the brain activates resilience. So, here comes the question: if you were to adopt a mind-set of resilience right now, how would you physically do it? Some of my clients imagine putting on a coat, others pretend to carry a shield on their arm, others a badge over their hearts. Whatever it is, it will need a physical motion from you to 'activate' it.

Once you have decided on what the physical activation motion is, stand up firm and straight and breathe deeply. Practice the motion until it feels comfortable and meaningful. Enjoy the feeling in your body of having activated resilience. Now think back to the event that knocked you off course. Play it over in your mind from your place of peak resilience. How does it feel? It ought to feel manageable, less emotive, and you ought to feel somewhat detached and calmer about it. Keep practicing the physical motion, get your heart rate up slightly and watch your body posture and breathing.

BE REMARKABLE IN ALL THAT YOU DO

Make an impact. Be memorable. Whether it is the depth of your expertise, your engaging style, or the magnetism of your passions, be someone who stands out for all the right reasons. This may sometimes mean that you have to take the road less travelled, or go against the grain. Taking a stand is admirable if done professionally and assertively, but with respect, kindness and compassion always.

Demonstrating strong qualities such as integrity and authenticity will also earn you admiration. It starts from having a strong personal identity, which even if subjected to criticism, ridicule or scorn, will leave you unscathed, because you know who you are and what you stand for. This steadfastness in turn creates a following. Whether you are a grandparent or a child genius – it's never too late. By being you, you will be imitated, admired and remembered. Your legacy will ignite the same qualities in the generations that follow you.

If you are in business, offer a product or service that gets people excited, that makes your employees feel proud (as Branson put it). Money does not buy remarkability so don't wait until you have it to be it. Challenge the status quo.

What you do with what you have amounts to being remarkable. Develop your edge!

SELF-RENEWAL IS PROFITABLE

Very often we deny ourselves the opportunity to 'renew' ourselves: we don't take nearly enough time out to think, relax, refresh products, improve services, re-engineer processes, upgrade technologies, or enhance marketing efforts. We perceive this as taking our foot off the pedal with consequential, often imaginary negative impacts. Time out may well result in a short term dip in potential earnings, but we fear that may be catastrophic.

Quite the opposite.

Stephen Covey describes it as taking time out to 'sharpen the saw' in the *7 Habits of Highly Effective People*. He describes the four areas of renewal as:

- The physical aspects of the body which include exercise, nutrition, rest, relaxation, and stress management
- The social and emotional aspects of displaying empathy,

being in service of others, synergy of thought and action, and seeking intrinsic security
- The spiritual elements of value clarification, commitment, study and undertaking meditative practices
- The mental investment of reading, visualising, planning and writing

We spend a lot of time perfecting our homes, or upgrading our cars. We buy new shoes and clothing, bags and skin-enhancing products. What exactly do we do with our minds? What investment in developing our minds have we really undertaken? Our studies, maybe the odd training course – it's not enough. It needs to be a continuous process.

Detaching from circumstances, creating space and reflecting objectively brings perspective. Ideas spring from the clearing of the mind, and this could be hugely profitable. It's an investment.

Self-renewal is a serious requirement. A major component of it is to create time to have fun! Schedule frequent time away from what you do if you have to, to remind you to laugh, unwind, and create happy memories. Having fun during the process of life is a must!

Why develop Enterprising behaviours?

Whether or not you are an entrepreneur, the entrepreneurial mindset is definitely something to replicate, given the challenges we are going to be faced with in the near future.

Here are just a few of the benefits of developing the behaviours of an entrepreneur.

It will give you a broader range of career options and income-generating streams. You will not accept suffering, the status quo, mediocrity or anything less than what is best for you. Entrepreneurial behaviours stimulate creative thinking. You will want to innovate, explore, expand your consciousness, and by so doing you will create value for yourself, your business, your family, society, people and causes you care about. You will learn how to assess and manage risk and you will also therefore take calculated risks, which in turn push out the boundaries and enable you to achieve things that you may not have otherwise ventured into. It will increase your capacity for handling change, making you more adept at thriving in ambiguous environments. This enhances your resilience and will reduce stress levels. You will develop a spirit of collaboration. Working together with other people will both inspire greatness and deliver an exponentially positive result.

What better reason can there be for developing entrepreneurial behaviours than feeling a greater sense of happiness and fulfilment from having invested your intellectual muscle and creative prowess in a meaningful solution?

How to develop Enterprising behaviours

Sounds wonderful, I know, but how does one develop those behaviours? Here are a few tips.

Working from your vision (Chapter Two), think about your strengths and weaknesses: what attributes do you currently have and what do you not have that you need to achieve your vision? Believe that you can achieve whatever you set out to. Practically speaking, you will have to address those skills and knowledge gaps, so immerse yourself in content – books, biographies, magazines, videos, online research.

Signing up for a course will ensure that you acquire knowledge and it will provide you with access to like-minded people on a similar journey but with different backgrounds and experience. More sophisticated programmes will include case studies, site visits, simulations, business games and experiential learning that will enable you to learn and practice entrepreneurial behaviours.

Attend networking events, seminars, business forums; contribute to blogs, and other social media. Learn about what similar people do, how they got started, what were some of their pitfalls. Develop that enquiring mind.

Do something creative that is aligned to your vision, e.g. artwork for your products, service, website, marketing materials; music for your promotional video; photography for your business or family.

Work with a mentor to help you get perspective, prioritise appropriately, obtain insights on where to focus. Work with a coach to reinforce your mind-set of steel.

Daniel Priestley, in his book *Entrepreneur Revolution: How to Develop Your Entrepreneurial Mindset and Start a Business That Works,* describes how to change the way you think, the way you network, and the way you make a living. He talks about how we all have an empire-building brain which we tend not to use because lower order brain functions are over-stimulated, for example when we see scarce resources we become selfish, adopt tunnel vision tendencies and our imagination diminishes. Other tendencies include focusing on repetitive work because we are good at it, rather than it being something of value. The empire builder is someone who is creative, strategic, and resourceful.

Are you an empire builder, even if it is a small empire to start off with?

These were just some ideas to prompt your thinking and encourage you to develop enterprising behaviours that underpin your success.

And finally, to continue the story of my entrepreneurial journey: for the avoidance of doubt, buying a $200,000 house off the internet without seeing it is not something I would advocate as demonstrating a desirable entrepreneurial quality, although in my case it worked out beautifully. In addition to being my personal place of renewal, the

Concordia Studio (my office on my premises), is also where transformations in my clients occur.

I am still, however, a student in the school of life. I constantly stumble and trip over things as I learn the art and science of exhibiting the behaviours of successful entrepreneurs. Rather than lick my wounds I've learned that the scars make for great war stories, which in themselves are empowering for me and for others. I have high tides and low tides – business is, after all, cyclical. Learning to refrain from making knee-jerk decisions during the low tides has been my greatest accomplishment thus far. Instead I've learnt how to create high waves from low tides, i.e. create high value to people who really need it, for instance by using the time doing charitable work.

What I've also begun to realise is that low tides are perfect as they are – they are opportunities for self-renewal. It's not always about converting them. Accepting them as they are is equally powerful. Make the most of those times. They're there to help you gain perspective.

If only I had realised this during the period that preceded our move back to South Africa. The toughest time of my life: excruciating pain, incapacity and vulnerability … a time that started with reaching for that cup, wondering about a suitcase, my mind constantly replaying the image of that child, my heart ripped to shreds. If only I knew at the time that even low periods have a purpose in life.

Thanks to a fundamental shift in mind-set I now love the highs and lows, albeit for very different reasons. I use the low-tides to refocus, rejuvenate, give myself permission to relax, have fun and laugh often. I am retired after all! I hope you will recognise your low-tides and use them well too. As importantly, I hope you will celebrate your high-tides, share them with people around you so that they too may be inspired to follow their dreams. Change happens one person at a time.

FIVE

ENHANCE EXPERTISE
THROUGH EDUCATION

'My mother said I must always be intolerant of ignorance but understanding of illiteracy. That some people, unable to go to school, were more educated and more intelligent than college professors,'

MAYA ANGELOU (1928 – 2014)

Before you skip this chapter thinking studying is not for you, or that you've been there, done that and got the t-shirt, I have a surprise for you. What I am describing might be conventional for some, but could be quite innovative or thought-provoking for others. Please read on. This chapter is inspired by some of my greatest teachers at school, in business, in life, all of whom played an incredibly significant role in shaping who I am today. I have vivid memories of them – their behaviours, their teaching style, the way in which they interacted with me. Not all were 'nice' teachers – some were tough, some pushed me hard, but I got so much value from them. I appreciate them now so much more than I did back then.

More people over the next 30 years will be graduated through education than since the beginning of time, according to UNESCO (United Nations Education, Scientific and Cultural Organisation), as quoted by Sir Ken Robinson, a visionary cultural leader, creativity expert and best-selling author whose view is that we are all born creative but we are educating people out of it. Sir Ken claims we are educating for a protracted university entrance and are missing the objective of helping our children get a fair chance at making something of our future. Einstein famously said that unless we are prepared to be wrong, we cannot be creative as we will not come up with anything original.

The UK Trades Union Congress General Secretary Frances O'Grady said, *'It's great that more businesses want to recruit. But with jobseekers outnumbering vacancies by four to one, it's hugely frustrating that across the UK a large number of jobs go unfilled because of local skills shortages.'* (BBC report, 2014).

The internet has provided us with a wealth of data at our finger-tips, and we are swimming in a sea of information. Whilst this has enhanced our knowledge, I believe it has blurred our focus, overwhelming us with too much choice, often conflicting, and too little time in which to make sound decisions. This has shifted us back into mere survival mode.

Many people do not have access to proper education. Some do, but do not rate education a priority; others recognise its importance but find it difficult to afford the escalating costs. Some people have re-mortgaged houses and taken unmanageable loans to finance their own and the studies of their loved ones; others have worked their way through an ivy-league education, believing it will secure their financial freedom in future. Even organisations are being challenged by governments to take more of an active role in investing in the development of their people, through the use of mechanisms such as Skills Development Levies – taxes levied by governments on business if they cannot evidence developing their staff. Certification and accreditation, whilst sometimes useful and other times laughable, have become an essential part of distinguishing the wheat from the chaff.

The topic of education evokes high emotion – sometimes incredulity at cost, sometimes pride at impact – but there's no avoiding it. An executive MBA programme in the US costs well over $100,000, whilst school fees at private schools in London can be upwards of £30,000 per student per year. Top primary schools in South Africa cost in the region of R100,000 per year per child. This is fine but inaccessible to the majority.

There is a flip side to this. I know that some of the greatest minds of the 21st century barely finished high school, or if they did, many of them dropped out of university as it limited their ability to create. Branson, Gates and Jobs are examples of this. There is also no guarantee that the most expensive educational institutions will achieve the best results.

The point is this: we need a hybrid approach to education. It is not just up to governments and the private sector, or the elite schools and universities with hefty price tags. It is about every one of us stretching the boundaries to educate ourselves, and all who come after us. Waiting for education systems to catch up will take too long. We need more than just formal education to develop the expertise needed for the future. So this chapter describes how to develop expertise in ourselves, our communities and our organisations. It is also about how to educate our children ourselves, using all available resources to develop the capabilities needed for the future so that we can actually build that future rather than perish in it.

'We need to learn how to use our minds well, and then we need to teach students how to do the same. Understanding how to identify and then scaffold the "habits of mind" that improve learning capability, is essential for the future. Whilst it is relatively difficult to predict the future and what the demands of the workforce will be, it is not difficult to predict that we will need to have people who have learned how to learn, who have an intellectual curiosity about the world around them and who are interested in seeking solutions where problems exist. That is the starting point.'

TREVOR NAIDOO, PRINCIPAL 2004-2012,

LANDMARK HIGH SCHOOL, NEW YORK CITY

What we have been educating for over the last 25 years has taken us slightly off course. The margin of error continues to grow with each year we leave things as they are. There is no point analysing where or why it went wrong; I am more interested in understanding what corrective measures we are now putting in place to achieve the outcomes we need for the future.

In my interview with Dr Adam Gordon, futurist and author of *Future Savvy: Quality in Foresight,* and Director of Executive and Corporate Education at one of South Africa's leading universities, he said,

'We are well aware of the challenges facing business in the next five to ten years. The rise of the global middle-class, their consumption patterns, their education and employment needs will place great demands on how we run business. We (at the University) are taking a continuous learning approach to developing leadership curricula that move away from functional competence and focus instead on the higher order functioning of critical thinking, reasoning, and immediate application of learning, exposing future world leaders to accelerated learning environments. We need these environments, the approach to learning and the embedding of skills to be replicated across all education stages, all facets of life and all aspects of work for this transformation in mind-set to be sustainable.'

We are faced with the stark reality of many graduates being either jobless or working in jobs they are not suited for. At the same time there are many people who believe they are not 'able' or *something* enough (e.g. good enough, smart enough) to go into a career they would like. What will it take to create a compelling enough proposition for people to make the shift in enhancing their expertise through a variety of educational sources in order to align their passions to what is needed for the future?

What expertise will be needed in future

There are numerous reports that inform us of the shortage of skills needed for the future.

In a survey of 91,000 employers, reported by the BBC in January 2014, *'the UK Commission for Employment and Skills found more than one in five vacancies were down to a poor skills base. The UKCES found 146,200 job vacancies (22%) in 2013 were unfilled because of inadequate skills, compared with 91,400 (16%) two years earlier. The UKCES report,* Skills for Sustainable Recovery, *amongst other things, suggests that the problem of inadequate skills, qualifications or experience in the workforce is hitting some industries harder than others, with more skills shortages found in areas such as manufacturing, construction and plumbing, as well as in health and social care. The study said employers struggled to find employees with the "core generic skills" of communication, literacy and numeracy. There has been an increase in the proportion of skill-shortage vacancies resulting from a lack of communication skills, particularly oral communication (41%, up from 37% in 2011), as well as a lack of literacy (34% up from 28% in 2011) and numeracy skills (26%, up from 24%). It also found nearly half of employers across the UK (48%) admitted to recruiting people with higher levels of skills and knowledge than were required for the job. College leavers were reported by employers to be more "work ready" than school leavers of the same age.'*

In addition, the Hay Group's *Global Talent Shortages Report* (2012) also highlights a shortage of soft skills, namely: *'the ability to speak another language other than English, the ability to work collaboratively in a team and communicate effectively, the ability to manage teams and demonstrate effective leadership traits and skills, and organisation skills to optimise efficiencies. They also list the following hard skill shortages: Finance & Budgeting, IT, Green Skills (energy and construction), Procurement and Negotiation, Research & Development, and Healthcare skills.'*

Having become aware of this issue, the UK government is now trialling solutions to enhance mathematics skills. Teachers from Shanghai will be brought to the UK to create 'maths hubs' which strengthen teaching capabilities, according to Elizabeth Truss, Education Minister, as reported by the BBC. *'The maths hubs will be partnerships of schools, which will work with maths experts and share best practice with other schools in their area, growing the interest and capabilities in students and most importantly making mathematics less abstract and more relevant to real life situations that children can relate to.'*

We know that in many countries there is a huge shortage of trades. Australia in particular reports needing a range of motor mechanic-related skills and a range of metal worker professions. The United Arab Emirates, as part of the significant development it has been undergoing in recent years, is investing in infrastructure and is insourcing construction 'skills' from neighbouring countries and large conglomerates in order to address in-country demand.

Farming is going to become a critically important profession in the next 20 years. Jim Rogers, renowned American Investor, as reported in the *Financial Times*, suggests that the average age of a farmer in the US is 58, in Korea it's 65. *'It is an old profession and the people in it are dying out or retiring. In the US, more people study public relations than agriculture. The world is facing a serious food production problem. If something doesn't change then we won't have food at any price.*

Prices will have to go up a lot to attract labour. In the past, if we had problems with the weather, then we had huge inventories. But now we don't have inventories and we don't have farmers. The world's population is expected to grow to 9 billion by 2040, and those extra two billion people are going to need quantities of food which are not yet being produced.'

There are conflicting reports about whether the quantities of food needed for the future can be produced or not. The fact that there are conflicting reports worry me – we need certainty. And the only way to achieve certainty is to attract more people to the profession to do the thinking around it. Despite knowing these challenges lie ahead, we continue to educate replicas of ourselves, with only marginal improvements. How exactly do we plan on addressing this problem? How will we get more children studying and excelling in maths and science, to create the solutions for fresh water supplies and alternative energy provision? How will we develop stronger business acumen, improved numeracy skills, critical thinking and better analysis skills, superior decision-making skills, and both a depth and breadth of expertise? Even though governments set the national curriculum, how do we get schools to expand what's on offer to include more arts, sports and trades? What are the roles of business and parents in this ecosystem?

Are we inadvertently consenting to the demise of our futures and our extinction? Are we leveraging the power of the brain well enough?

How does learning take place in the brain?

The brain is more powerful than any supercomputer on the planet. It comprises three main areas: the brain stem, the cerebellum and the cerebrum. The brain stem is responsible for regulating the cardiac, respiratory and central nervous functions and it maintains consciousness including monitoring the sleep cycle. The cerebellum is responsible for motor control, co-ordination and precision. The cerebrum is most important for learning as this is where memory and reasoning occur. Each area of the cerebrum specialises in a sensory processing function. Learning happens when sensory input is transmitted through a network of neurons via nerve impulses. There are over 100 billion neurons in the brain and each neuron can make up to 15,000 connections with other neurons through synaptic contacts. The information is then held in short term memory. It is compared with existing memories stored in long term memory and instantaneously decisions on reaction to the stimuli and retention of the memory are made. Depending on the nature of the stimulus, transmission may be affected. For example, if it is a new experience, then new synapses will have to connect, taking a little while longer and possibly not remembering the incident fully. For example, if your wallet was snatched, the shock of the incident causes new neural pathways to form, but as they do, you may not remember every fine detail of the incident.

Learning is achieved through the strengthening of neural pathways, which occur through frequent connections of brain cells. Researchers at the University of California Irvine's Centre for the Neurobiology of Learning and Memory found that when two neurons communicate more often, they form a bond enabling information to be transmitted faster and more accurately. This results in more complete memories and easier recollection, especially if the experience is more recent. In another recent study at the Martinos Centre for Biomedical Imaging, Department of Radiology, the Massachusetts General Hospital and Harvard Medical School found that if we experience an emotional reaction to an incident, that emotion becomes wired to that memory and strengthens it dramatically, including strengthening recollection of the event.

What this is telling us is that we have to engage all senses to stimulate emotion around learning, in order for it to be memorable and impactful.

What other educational options are there?

Start early with educating your children as in Chapter Three and Four. Sarah Jane Blakemore is a cognitive neuroscientist who studies the 'network' of regions in the brain involved in understanding other people, specifically in adolescents. According to her, synaptic shedding (the loss of brain cells in the grey matter of the prefrontal cortex of the adolescent brain) occurs as a result of under-use in adolescence. Shedding enables those synapses already in use to strengthen. Therefore exposing your child early to learning opportunities improves brain development.

If you are an educator, teacher, parent or guardian, your role is critical going forward. Approach it with zest and passion – you are influencing the most important aspect of our future: our children. Spark in them a yearning for positivity, growth, and contribution. Socrates was put on trial for 'corrupting the youth' because he taught a method of rational inquiry: learning through asking questions. American educator Geoffrey Canada has done incredible work for over 20 years with the Harlem Children's Zone (HCZ). His goal was to increase high school and college graduation rates amongst its students. The HCZ is an organisation that provides high-quality education to children in a large area of Harlem, New York and aims to follow the academic career of its students. The documentary *Waiting for Superman* (2010) was based on Canada, and he himself featured prominently. Film critic Roger Ebert wrote: '*What struck me most of all was Geoffrey Canada's confidence that… a good education… is not ruled out by poverty, uneducated parents or crime and drug-infested neighbourhoods. In fact, those are the very areas where he has success.*'

Another earlier example of an extraordinary educator is Anne Sullivan (1866-1936). Although some time ago, she became famous for teaching Helen Keller, who had been both deaf and blind since she was one year old, how to communicate effectively. Sullivan overcame these obstacles by teaching Keller the alphabet through the sense of touch – touching the objects and then spelling words into the girl's hands.

The lesson to be learned from these inspiring teachers is that they rose above it all by personal choice; they surpassed all barriers and constraints. They taught from a place of abundance. They knew no limits. They nurtured the infinite minds of others. So can you. Encourage the 'enquiring mind' concept, in the mode of Maria Montessori, the Italian medical doctor and education reformer (1870-1952), whose 'discovery' education focuses on the child's independence and psychological development path. Asking questions, challenging rationale, encouraging critical thinking and exploring creative solutions are the cornerstones of this approach.

Excellent communication skills, both written and verbal are going to be an essential requirement for the future. Linked to this is the need to encourage people to learn a different language. Romantic languages will always have their charm but it's time to prioritise and really get focused – the east is going to become the engine room for many parts of business, so learning Mandarin, Japanese or Korean may be more useful and challenging. Children have a wonderful ability to pick up languages when they are young, so they must be encouraged to do so early on. This is because the cerebral cortex is at a critical stage of development and its 'plasticity' enables more words and structures (different languages) to be learned.

Expose children to technology early and even if somehow *you've* managed to escape it up to now, it's time for you to face the online world. There is a whole raft of benefits to be gained by improving computer literacy skills. Increasingly, nursery schools are using iPads and tablets with their toddlers. Even if you don't know or own the technology yourself, don't have broadband or wi-fi in the area that you live in, or the money to afford it, take young children to places where they will have exposure to people who have them and who can help them. Libraries and community centres will be good places to start if your children are not yet of school-going age. Do whatever it takes (legally and safely) to gain exposure to these technologies.

We can no longer educate for deep 'singular' expertise. There has to be a depth and breadth to skills and knowledge in the future. No longer can you survive being either a specialist or a generalist. The ideal profile for the future is a term I would like to coin: 'Expergens' – expert generalists who have deep specialisms in a variety of in-demand content areas.

'A critical leadership challenge is how to create and retain the emotional heartbeat of the organisation,'
DOUGLAS UMBERS, MD AND LEADER OF WORLD CLASS,
TECHNOLOGY-ENABLED SERVICE ORGANISATIONS, 2014.

Irrespective of your field of specialism, you will need to develop key leadership skills such as business acumen, decisiveness, and conflict management. This requires enhanced mental faculties and memory so we will find increasing numbers of younger people leading companies, despite having less experience, because they will exercise superior cognitive ability than the older generations as they access, process, recall, and analyse greater volumes of information faster, and are more aggressive and tenacious with implementing change to achieve desired results.

Robert Kiyosaki's *Rich Dad Poor Dad* series of educational books and CDs go a long way in helping parents teach their children financial concepts from an early age. His 'Cashflow' board and software games for adults and children have received excellent reviews in helping parents teach their children financial concepts from an early age.

Improving memory is also going to be a feature of the future. You can improve your memory by adopting techniques like the Linking System to remember lists. It uses stories, symbols, humour and other interesting items to help you remove the randomness of lists, and instead create a relationship between each item. You could also extrapolate on the list by visualising and adding colour to the items. The wackier the visual imagery the more memorable the list.

Similarly, there are techniques for remembering numbers. Chunking large numbers into groups of two to four numbers at a time helps, and reading them accordingly makes the brain *feel* like it has to recall 'less'. For example the number 56834971969012 could be read like 56 83 497 1969 012 and spoken as fifty-six, eighty-three / four, ninety seven / nineteen, sixty nine / oh, twelve. You could also associate certain numbers to significant dates, events or people. For example the 012 could be a telephone dialling area code; 1969 could have been a famous year; 56 may be someone's age; 83 may be a house number.

Another system, called the Peg System, may prove useful. It assigns a picture to represent each of the 10 key numbers and enables you to recall the number through a story. Here's an example, and you can change the imagery to suit you:

0 = a coin
1 = a flagpole
2 = a swan
3 = a triangle
4 = a roof
5 = a hook

6 = a golf club
7 = an axe
8 = a snowman
9 = a balloon on a string

So the number 8429 could be the story of a snowman, who hooked the roof of a house to a swan that carried it away with the help of a balloon on a string. Sounds a little ridiculous, I know, and takes some getting used to, but is helpful when recalling telephone numbers, pin-codes and dates.

These are just a few basic memory enhancing techniques already in use today. For what is needed in future, there is some catching up to do!

Another option to consider in alternative education is leveraging the strengths of multi-generational workforces. Experience shows that there can be high tensions in a workplace, due to mixed values and differing styles of working, but this is also a great opportunity to leverage strength from diversity. The older generation is steeped in values such as loyalty and perseverance; they may be less techno-savvy but are usually great communicators. Keeping able-bodied older people in employment has positive health impacts, pension provisions are redeemed later, and it will enable mentoring of the younger generations.

Another way to deepen expertise is through immersion. Reading books, undertaking internet-based research, self-study of subjects of interest, attending conferences, and listening to podcasts are all forms of deepening knowledge and expertise. Learning is embedded by sharing it with others; surrounding oneself with like-minded people will spark ideas and will foster highly rewarding experiences.

Unless you use what you have learnt, you will lose the memory of it. A famous Chinese proverb goes, '*Tell me and I will forget, show me and I may remember, involve me and I will understand.'* A prime example of this is to share what you've learned on every forum possible. Formulate an opinion, test it with others, start conversations, create a buzz, start a following, get famous. For example, you could speak about a topic of interest at your school or university, or in the workplace if you are a business professional. You could write articles, publish them on blogs and other social media sites. Take knowledge and skills acquisition into your own hands. Harvard and Yale Universities, amongst others, offer free courses online through MOOCs, massive open online courses. Lectures and course material are available on the internet at no charge, and I hope that this trend not only continues but expands – with more universities and educational institutions supplying courses and material online so that people have access to information which increases their curiosity, and informs their study and career choices. Oxford University and other prestigious learning institutions offer affordable online programmes. Read, research and engage with online resources, contribute to discussions, broaden content horizons. The key is to begin this as early as possible, i.e. from when a child starts school. Studying an advanced subject of interest from childhood in parallel to basic schooling will go a long way in preparing for the future. Whatever your age, you're old enough to start now.

Enhancing expertise is attained through repetition. Malcolm Gladwell in his book *Outliers* claims that the key to success in any field is, to a large extent, a matter of practising a specific task for 10,000 hours or more. Younger people need more encouragement, recognition and acknowledgement to develop expertise in something they show an interest in. As life gets busier and fuller we tend to forget to celebrate accomplishments often enough, especially the small ones, not just for children but for each other as adults too. It's important. We are social creatures. What gets rewarded gets repeated.

Source help from specialists. Whether you are a high school student needing extra lessons, an entrepreneur needing a business coach, a business professional needing a mentor, or an organisation insourcing specialist skills, learning from people with more experience and deeper skills is an accelerated way to prepare for the challenges of the future.

We need to take a longer term approach to developing expertise. What I've described requires each individual to take initiative for themselves and for their children.

Another dimension to enhancing expertise is by getting corporates to invest in talent development at grassroots level. Already, large conglomerates go into schools to create awareness and encourage students to take specific courses. Consulting firms also spend significant sums of money marketing consulting careers to students at high school and university levels. More of this needs to be done. We have to invest in the present to guarantee our future – and more and more businesses are realising this. Additional entrepreneurial programmes and trades like electrical, plumbing and construction need to be introduced in school curriculums. Community development centres also need to support these efforts if schools (through governments) are unable to make it to the party on time. Organisations need to also get creative with their apprenticeship programmes.

Many foundations are committed to providing additional opportunities for less advantaged people: the Cherie Blair Foundation for Women (CBFW) mentors female entrepreneurs around the world; the Oprah Winfrey Leadership Academy for Girls teaches disadvantaged girls a range of skills; the Richard Branson Centre of Entrepreneurship encourages entrepreneurial minds; the Bill & Melinda Gates Foundation supports initiatives in education, healthcare and the impacts of population growth by providing grants to initiatives that deliver sustainable global change. At the heart of these foundations is people who have heart; people who care enough to do more than just make money for themselves. You don't need to be a multimillionaire to make a contribution to life. It's as easy as volunteering your time, teaching a skill that you have, or providing support to a disadvantaged family in your community. For me education is not about intellect – it is about extending the best of yourself.

Put into practice and keep practising the skill you want to acquire. Don't wait for the permission, qualification, badge, symbol or sign to start being your best you. Be bold. Just start being your best self from the point of decision. Constantly repeating the skill or behaviour makes it a habit. Repetition is the key to developing mastery.

The focus is not just about developing deep and wide expertise; it needs to be developed in areas of passion, aligned to the needs of the new world. Most people would love a career in day-dreaming, but sadly there's no future in that. It is essential to consider what you could be famous for, what specialist skill or knowledge you can offer to the market and how that will make you an indispensable component of the ecosystem in which you function.

One income stream will no longer be sufficient in the new world, so learning how to channel your passions and transform them into passive income streams will be an important requirement of the future. David Beckham is a great example of capitalising on his personal brand and diversifying into other fields. The ex-English footballer continues to enjoy sponsorships and endorsements from major organisations like Adidas and Armani even though he is now retired. He has his own fashion and fragrance ranges which deliver a steady income stream.

With the change in employment models, critical skills will be retained in an organisation and other organisational roles will be outsourced to the free market. There will be little merit in continuing with outsourced providers because of the overhead costs and management fees. Instead, could www.fiverr.com become 'the' resourcing model of the future? And if so, how do you cleverly survive on $5 per job?

Some universities partner with high schools, exposing them to the foundation levels of parts of the curriculum. Columbia University in the US partnered with Landmark High School in Manhattan some years ago; Cambridge University in the UK partners with Ashton College in Johannesburg. This practice needs to grow in order to bridge the gap in the levels of education and the degree of sophistication between school and university education. We need to accelerate the development of skills and knowledge so that it is immediately applicable to the working world.

Why enhance expertise?

Studies have shown that people with poor numeracy skills are more than twice as likely to be unemployed as those exhibiting high degrees of numeracy. Consequently, *'a quarter of young people in custody in several states in the US, have a numeracy level below that expected of a seven-year-old, and 65% of adult prisoners have numeracy skills at or below the level expected of an 11-year-old. Interestingly, 14-year-olds who had poor numeracy skills at age 11 are more than twice as likely to play truant as those achieving the expected skills at age 11,'* reports the National Numeracy Charity in the UK.

This is not a matter of choice. It has become compulsory. If we are to cultivate the next generation of innovators and leaders, we need to accelerate development and learning, and foster the development of the brain to meet the challenges of the new world. If we are able to think at a higher level sooner, increase our mental processing speed and memory, we will have developed a maturity in cognitive ability that equips us for the business world sooner.

Schools and universities are not going to be able to deliver this on time. So I need your help, right now. Think of a teenager in your life and what you believe they are capable of. Now do two things. Do something for them that kick-starts this new path of development for them, e.g. send them a book, or an article, or source a university prospectus. Then pick up the phone and tell them that you believe in them; offer your help; point out their positive qualities. Leave them motivated, inspired – you may have just sparked something in them that makes a difference. Make the call on our future by making that phone call today.

SIX

EMOTIONAL INTELLIGENCE

'The third decade of emotional intelligence is about application. These are the foundational skills for human interaction, so in this third decade we'll see emotional intelligence woven more deeply and powerfully into the fabric of our institutions and lives. It's time not just to know, or to value but to practice.'

JOSHUA FREEDMAN (QUOTED IN 2014)

Emotional Intelligence as a concept has been around from as far back as Marcus Aurelius' reign 161 – 180AD. He was noted for saying, *'Let no emotions of the flesh, be they of pain or of pleasure, affect the supreme and sovereign portion of the soul. See that it never becomes involved with them; it must limit itself to its own domain, and keep the feelings confined to their proper sphere.'* More recently, in the 1800s, Charles Darwin and others believed that emotional expression was essential for survival. Alfred Binet, in the late 1800s, developed what is thought to be the first intelligence test. In the 1940's psychologist David Wechsler created the Wechsler Adult Intelligence Scale (WAIS), a test designed to measure intelligence in older adolescents and adults. Howard Gardner's book in 1983, *Frames of Mind: The Theory of Multiple Intelligences*, articulated seven criteria for a behaviour to be considered an intelligence. Pioneering use of the term 'emotional intelligence' is attributed to a doctoral thesis by Wayne Payne in 1985:

A Study of Emotion: Developing Emotional Intelligence. Psychologists Peter Salovey and John Mayer in 1990 also put forward an ability-oriented model of emotional intelligence to process emotional information and use it to navigate social environments.

Their work paved the way for Daniel Goleman who, in 1995, defined emotional intelligence as a wide array of skills and competencies that improve performance, enhance leadership skills and enable greater mental health. Goleman to this day remains the authority on emotional intelligence. Goleman's model, described in his article entitled, 'What Makes A Leader' (*Harvard Business Review*, 1998), defines the following five constructs:

1. Self-awareness – the ability to know one's emotions, strengths, weaknesses, drives, values and goals, and recognise their impact on others while using gut feelings to guide decisions.
2. Self-regulation – controlling or redirecting one's disruptive emotions and impulses and adapting to changing circumstances.
3. Social Skill – managing relationships to move people in the desired direction
4. Empathy – considering other people's feelings, especially when making decisions
5. Motivation – being driven to achieve for the sake of achievement.

Emotional intelligence has been a prominent component of developing leaders over the last 20 years. It is the single biggest predictor of workplace performance and the strongest driver of leadership and personal excellence. Studies show that top performers and high earners scored well in emotional intelligence tests. It surprises me that a significant number of people and organisations do not give it credence, have not adopted it and continue to debate it.

This chapter is not about assessing where we are on the scale of adopting emotional intelligence and why. It is not about encouraging the merits of Daniel Goleman's model either. That's old news. Emotional intelligence is here to stay. Instead, this chapter is about its evolution, the 'next stage' of emotional intelligence, which is essential in helping us achieve the shift in mind-set needed for the future, starting now.

The Mind Age™ – 5 Forces Framework for the Future
In keeping with my love of physics, and my deep admiration for Isaac Newton, I believe that Goleman's five constructs need to evolve into something more forceful for the future, in order to have the impact that is needed to provoke change. I have named my recommendations for the next stage of emotional intelligence, the '5-Forces Framework for the Future', and it is depicted below.

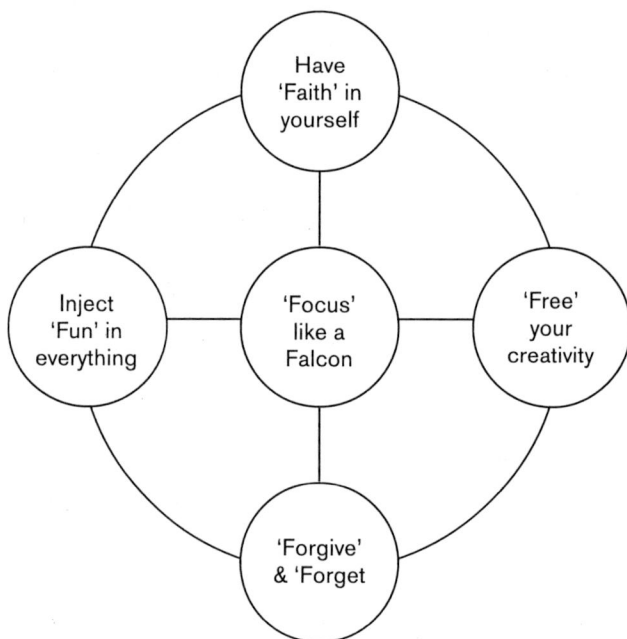

This chapter describes each of the 5 Forces that I believe we will need to master emotionally so as to live productive lives:

Faith in self: develop an unfaltering sense of self-belief and self-mastery

Many people find themselves drowning in a sea of doubt and insecurity. They also find themselves in the company of people who keep them down, reinforcing their low sense of self-worth. Operating from this space means what little confidence you may have or be able to muster, haemorrhages in no time. Such people wallow in the belief that they are not worthy or good enough, and this can lead to feelings of being an 'impostor' or a fraud in what they do. The behaviour that stems from this belief is self-sabotage, creating the vicious cycle of failing, which reinforces the belief that they cannot be successful. The misery and suffering that results from this pattern of behaviour leave people feeling incapacitated. The turmoil derived from the inner conflict of needing to change but not feeling able to, plunges them into the shadows of uncertainty. Analysing the early life causes of these feelings brings little value to making the decision to change. Emotionally intelligent people of the future do not deal in regrets, so I want to help you build a strong sense of self-belief, if you do too.

At the opposite end of the spectrum is another type of person who appears to gush self-belief. They are loud, domineering, they sound authoritative and claim to be an expert, all of which is fine, except for the give-aways: they are high-strung, short-tempered and intense. Do not confuse the 'sound' of such people with their ability to deliver genuine value or impart real expertise. In many cases it is simply a mask to hide insecurity or a wall to keep you away. This is not the model for people with high emotional intelligence.

If you recognise yourself in one of these two scenarios, or feel that you may be somewhere in between on the spectrum, here are a few ways to cultivate self-belief.

HOW TO CULTIVATE SELF-BELIEF AND ACHIEVE SELF-MASTERY
Find something to write on or in.

Ask yourself the following questions: What is your self-image? How do you see yourself? How do you feel about yourself? Write it down at the very top of the page.

Now divide your page into three columns.

Think a negative thought about yourself. Yes you read right. Now think about a few more negative feelings and beliefs and make a list of them in the left hand column. Leave enough space between each item. For example, you may feel like you are not smart enough to study, or not good enough for that promotion, or not attractive enough for that person to be attracted to you.

Against each of the negative thoughts, feelings and beliefs, write down evidence to dispute them in the middle column. For example, list all your achievements, all the feedback you have received, and all the compliments you may have received in the past. This helps somewhat with the rational side of the brain processing facts against false beliefs. Re-examine the first column and challenge yourself as to how true these statements *really* are. Strike off those that are not true.

In the final column, for those statements that survived the Pinocchio test, rephrase your negative thoughts, feelings and beliefs using positive language. For example, '*Not being very good at working on computers gives me an opportunity to learn, after which I will have the appropriate skills for jobs that I apply for.*' Another example could be, '*Telling people off is a sign of inner confidence which I now recognise I have, but I now know I need to channel it in a more respectful way to yield the outcome I want.*'

Once you've captured your thoughts, review everything you have written.

Now take your own side. Back yourself. Become 'pro' you! Sometimes people actually side against themselves. I am an expert in this subject – I used to be one of those people! It led to horrible paths of self-destruction and self-perpetuating misery. We tend to side with the negative self-talk and almost fracture our personalities to keep us stuck in misery. Choose the side you are going to back. And then decide whether you are going to champion your own cause, or cheer for the 'other' side, i.e. your small sense of self. It's simply a choice. There is no mind exercise to go with this part of the process.

Focus on the positive evidence you have written down and allow your emotions to surface. I know this may be difficult as your own negative talk gets in the way. Keep working on it. Whereas the step above was about developing a list of objective evidence, this step is about allowing yourself to feel good about the evidence. Allow it to envelop you. Focus on the aspects of yourself that you value. Show gratitude for it – compliment yourself, start a gratitude journal and record empowering events or thoughts in it, keep doing more of the same to increase the frequency of that feel good feeling. Affirmations or mantras are also a great way of reinforcing positive belief patterns.

I mentioned earlier that you need to source feedback from others. This is helpful initially when reviewing the rational evidence, but at this stage you need to move away from needing constant feedback to make you feel better. Feedback must not become a fix. It will make you become a pleaser, which is not sustainable, and does not honour the essence of who you are. I don't want you to be under any illusion that feedback is the goal – it is not. This process enables you to integrate emotion with logic, making for a convincing shift in how you regard yourself. In your heightened state of positivity, elevate your thinking to higher order priorities. Rise above the mundaneness of day-to-day whinging, worrying, complaining, and procrastinating. Decide who you are when operating from your higher self, and define what that looks, sounds and feels like. If you aren't already, imagine yourself working alongside or for someone you truly admire, and someone who believes in you. How would that change your modus operandi, your behaviours, your style of being? Imagine a life without petty annoyances, and visualise how free you will be if you were to operate from a space of importance, i.e. that you have to focus only on important matters.

Please note, this is not an invitation to arrogance, ignorance or avoidance. This is not about abdicating responsibility. Far from it. Instead, empower yourself to focus on the big ticket items that make a positive difference in your life. The longer you are able to stay focused on the positives, the closer you will be to achieving self-mastery.

Staying focused requires willpower – it spurs you forward. Perseverance is about staying the course despite the odds. Self-mastery is the ability to manage and effortlessly exhibit these qualities. It is primarily about adopting an attitude of confidence in your ability to handle anything that comes your way. This may mean that you build something regular into your schedule in the beginning that reinforces a positive mind-set, positive feelings and empowering beliefs. Mastery is only possible through repetition. What you enjoy gets repeated. So what is it that you need to master? How do you get to enjoy it first, in order to want to do it repeatedly? There can be no doubt when you are operating from a place of infallible self-belief. Questions like, *'Can I do this?'*, *'What if I don't know enough?'*, *'What if I fail?'*, *'What will other people think of me?'*, *'Am I deserving?'* keep us in limbo. Switch the focus of the questions. Ask instead: *'How can I do this better/faster?'*, *'What additional input do I need and from whom?'*, *'What extra checks do I need to build in to mitigate risk?'*,

'Which stakeholders do I need to manage?', 'How will I celebrate my success?'

Do you notice the change?

Confidence is best described as someone who is willing to stand for what they believe in despite the consequences or criticism; someone who takes calculated risks to achieve better; someone who sees pitfalls as learning, never failures; someone who never shows off and accepts compliments humbly. What is most evident, however, is their style of communicating. Please do not be fooled by hyped-up crowd-pleasers who bamboozle us into believing or buying something we would not otherwise have. They offer very little substance and resort to this approach to mask the emptiness. Similarly, do not underestimate the quietly confident specialist who delivers value. Instead focus on what you need.

Some might think it naïve to envision a world where everyone radiates self-belief by 2040. Personally, I don't see why it should not be possible. My clients experience phenomenal breakthroughs during coaching, make life-changing decisions instantaneously and move forward with gusto. We are born with self-belief, and with every year of our life it erodes, for many of us, for all the wrong reasons. As parents we need to help our children maintain this sense of self-belief and as adults we simply need to reconnect with our 'knowing'. Only then is self-mastery possible.

Freedom: liberate yourself and empower others

For too long people have been chained to constructs that limited their potential. Fears, insecurities and limiting beliefs held them back from true self-expression. Nowadays, organisational structures, policies and personalities have also impeded progress. Stress, unreasonable demands and conflicting priorities place pressure on our ability to cope. People feel overwhelmed and resort to coping mechanisms and addictive tendencies like smoking, drinking alcohol, gambling, and over-eating to alleviate the perceived pressures and fears. Whatever the reasons, however legitimate, these behaviours cannot continue into the future.

Some organisations are already reaping the benefits of allowing their employees more freedom. For example, Google's '20% time' policy encourages its employees to spend 20% of their time pursuing a Google-related project; to date this has birthed several new Google products, and accounts for approximately 25% of their revenue. Similarly, an Australian company called Atlassian has implemented 'ShipIt' days based on a similar concept, committed to delivering value for their customers.

Andrew Crossey, Senior Vice President and Group Talent Director at Capgemini Consulting, says that idea generation must not be underestimated or neglected in the future.

'It's not just about encouraging employees to come up with ideas, but organisations have to invest in the infrastructure to bring those ideas to life. Innovation boards must not be made up of senior people. It will dry up ideas, and employees will auction the ideas or take them elsewhere. Get them involved in implementing their ideas. Acknowledge employees publically and share in the success of the idea. People need not be afraid to give up their ideas, and allow others to carry them forward if they are unable to. We live in a selfish way currently – we need to apply abundance thinking to how we operate in future.

It is also about time. We are increasingly feeling the pressures of needing to do more work, with greater complexity in less time. Technology is in a race to catch up with the demands of a consumer-centric world. However, going forward the emphasis must no longer be on speed, but instead how effectively we use time. For example, if telephone calls and wi-fi were readily available on long-haul flights, this could potentially negate the need for high speed transportation at high prices. This redefines what freedom means and enables.'

Having the freedom liberates us from the constraints that held us back in the past. Freedom is as much a state of mind as a condition of the environment in which you find yourself. We have to work from our best for this next era of our existence. Anything less will not cut it. We've done well over the last 25 years, but staying on this path for the next 25 years will just produce more of the same. It is not enough.

HOW TO FREE YOURSELF FROM THE CHAINS OF FEAR

People hold back because of a variety of fears. In some cases fears are generational – passed down from grandparents to parents to children. Very often fear is undefined: people fear fear itself. Fear can sometimes be amplified: a negative experience may have produced heightened fear, and by replaying the incident neural pathways increase and strengthen, and stress chemicals such as cortisol are released, thereby increasing the intensity of fear and anxiety. Fear prepares the body to react to danger. Adrenaline sharpens certain functions like eyesight and readies the body to deal with the perceived threat.

'I felt fear myself more times than I can remember, but I hid it behind a mask of boldness. The brave man is not he who does not feel afraid, but he who conquers that fear.'

NELSON MANDELA (1918 – 2013)

I have worked with several clients whose fear of failure and rejection had blocked them from taking that first or next step toward that 'something they've always wanted to do'. It invariably came from a deep insecurity linked to their self-esteem. In order for me to help them, I had to face my own fears, so I tried various techniques: from imagining the worst, rationalising the fear, assigning cartoon characters to the fear to minimise its impact, immersing myself in the fear, and other emotional management techniques (described in more detail in Chapter 9). Hypnosis did not work for me, so I did not recommend it to clients. I read every book possible on the subject, and found the perspectives of Susan Jeffers and Iyanla Vanzant easiest to relate to and most effective in addressing fears. They talked about making fear your friend. For me, in the end, all it took was a golf club and a stern talking to myself.

My defining moment with fear came when Shakeer was away on business for a week, and Jazzy, Lucy, Riley and I were alone at home one stormy night in Johannesburg. Riley was the latest addition to our family. He is a Swiss Shepherd dog and is tall and majestic. Despite being so large he is extremely quiet and quick in getting around. He looks scary at first glance but that makes *me* feel safe. On that particular night, every creak, squeak and rustle caused the dogs to run off in different directions barking uncontrollably, exacerbating my life-long fear of being alone and being attacked. After years of seeing someone in the shadows, losing sleep, having nightmares and thinking the worst, I decided that I had had enough. I dug out my Wellies (rubber Wellington boots), plonked on a hat and armed myself with a golf club. I flung the doors open and charged outside in the wind, rain and cold to get rid of the imaginary intruder who would come rustling by every house I lived in, irrespective of which city I was in, almost every night of my life. I shouted hysterically, taunting him out of hiding, swinging my golf club like a trained samurai. Lucy and Jazzy watched from a safe distance inside the house. Riley accompanied me with sheer delight, jumping up to catch as many raindrops in his mouth as possible. He kept a safe distance from me, smart enough to know that it would only be me getting hurt that night not least because I was a dangerously inexperienced golfer! After marching a few times around the house, drenched, completely fired up with adrenaline and ready to take on an army of intruders, I turned to the skies, shouting, *'Now listen here, Fear. I am done with you. You are either my friend or my foe. I need you to help me point out where the real dangers are, and I need to trust you to do this. Otherwise I have no use for you in my life. So now you choose!'* With that, I turned, and as I did I heard a rustle. I turned to face the direction in which it came from, poised with my club, feeling more like a mouse than a ninja, but I was determined to not run away. This huge figure leapt out of the bush, knocking me over, his full weight pinning me down. I struggled, desperately trying to break free, but to no avail. I was trapped face down, choking in the mud. My life flashed before my eyes, but soon stopped as I realised it was Riley! He thought it was a new game of night-time hide and seek in the rain. Fortunately neither of us was injured, although I looked a sight as I marched back into the house. Catching a glimpse of my scary appearance in the hallway mirror, I stopped and stared at myself. Just in case the intruder was hiding inside, I growled, *'Don't mess with me!'* And that was how I trained my dragon.

Something shifted in my mind that day. I had gotten to the end of my tether with this fear. Fear began to play a new role in my life from that night onward: part friend, part protector. I realised that wielding the golf club in the dark, in the rain and the wind was purely a gesture to programme my mind. The words shouted out loud just reinforced the association and created a new pattern of behaviour for reacting to fear. And if that intruder dares to make an appearance in future, well, I will be ready. Whatever it is, I can handle it. I wouldn't recommend to anyone the golf club or shouting at the skies in a storm to address fears, but I do recommend a tough conversation followed by some action.

Since then a deep instinct stirs in me when I need to pay special attention to something, or if I am in danger. Maybe it is just a coincidence that I sensed a pick-pocket targeting me one day. He approached me. I turned sharply toward him and said, *'If you are hungry, I will buy you food, but this wallet is mine.'* He looked at me shocked, then turned and walked away. I guess he was a reasonable man.

On another day I noticed I was being followed, so I turned around and started following him. It caught him off-guard, especially as I was wearing my favourite jumper with 'FBI' written across it.

My greatest 'knowing' was the time I hesitated for six seconds longer than I needed to at a traffic light. In Johannesburg this is virtually intolerable. I heard horns honking behind me. I raised my hand apologetically but I still stalled, not knowing why, fear gripping my heart like an icy hand. As I began to take off, an 18-wheeler truck ran a red light at what felt like 100 miles an hour at the intersection I was about to drive through. The horns continued to honk, but for a different reason this time.

Call it intuition or divine intervention, I hope this encourages you to fish out your fears, face them and befriend them. It is time to train your dragon. There is no place for fear in future, unless you need it as fuel. Fear is the lack of faith. Know your fear and have faith in yourself.

Focus: adopt the Falcon's force of focus

Sometimes life deals us a blow. It knocks us off-course. It's tough to get back up again. Sometimes people lack focus, or they lose focus quite easily. A combination of a lack of certainty, distractions, competing priorities, peer pressure and other behaviour dilutes focus.

This leaves people feeling like they accomplished nothing, or that what they accomplished was not good enough.

Slightly controversial, I know, using the predatory nature of the falcon as a means to imparting the importance of focus. Here's why I love falcons.

Falcons are able to fly at an extremely high altitude. This enables them to obtain a wider view of the surroundings, assess risks more objectively and get a clearer perspective. Once they spot their prey, they go into a cork-screw nose-dive, at incredible speeds of 200+ miles / 320+ kms per hour, making them the fastest creatures on earth. Diving this way enables them to maintain line of sight of their prey at all times. They hold focus, despite the height, and whilst flying at the breakneck speed. They strike their prey in mid-air, and if the speed and impact do not kill the prey on the first blow, the falcon will return time and again. Perseverance.

What is most interesting for me, however, is that the falcon is unafraid to tackle something as much as three or four times its size. Survival is instinctual, it gives them the courage to tackle something bigger than they are, purely to survive. These are exactly the techniques and tenacity that I believe we need to adopt from now on.

There will always be conflicts in our lives that detract our focus. Identifying them and learning how to stay focused in spite of them, will be essential for what we will need for the future. Too often we make excuses. We abandon a thought prematurely, or we give up too easily. Challenges exist to build commitment. They make for a fulfilling experience. They are necessary to keep us interested. Reframe challenges to help you maintain a strong sense of focus. Can you afford to be distracted from your life plan? If *you* don't achieve your life goals, who will? Conflicting priorities will always prevail. The key to success is to use conflict as a means of building character.

It is critical to define the priorities. Whereas envisioning provides us with the map of where we are going and the action plan to achieve it, we still need to identify the critical path: the list of priorities. Organising them into what is urgent and important is key to maintaining focus.

Conflict comes about when we try to do too much, when we are distracted from our priorities or when we have competing priorities. Feelings of overwhelm or even apathy descend upon us. It is important therefore to give ourselves enough time and enough challenge to stay focused. Too much or too little of each and we let go.

There is also the very real conflict of clashing with one or more people. This could be caused by a variety of reasons: differences in opinion, differences in approach, timing, urgency, personalities, hierarchies, and many other reasons. The Thomas-Kilmann Conflict Mode Instrument (TKI) helps identify preferred tendencies from the five styles they have identified – the competitive, collaborative, compromising, accommodating and avoiding styles. It is useful to identify your style, but remember people generally hate conflict, and will avoid it at all costs, or will instigate and never truly resolve it.

That's the old way of being.

Going forward, there is no avoiding the fact that you will disagree with people. Remove the antagonism from the conversation and just deal with the issue. Depersonalise it, defuse the emotion, remove the contention. Just work on resolving it. The first times may be tough going. A few more times and you will be an expert. Most importantly, a few more times after that and I predict… that there will be no need for conflict. It will simply become a conversation.

More organisations, universities and other private organisations are realising the need to have conflict resolution programmes in place. Universities including Cornell, Georgetown, Johns Hopkins and

George Mason have a range of undergraduate all the way through to doctoral level qualifications on conflict resolution. The Netherlands, Israel and India are investing in university programmes to create the skills needed to manage conflict effectively both now and in future. We have to achieve a step-change in how we manage conflict going forward. It can no longer be acceptable to go to war over anything, anymore. There is no justification for innocent lives being caught in the cross-fire of disagreements that erupt into wars. It has to stop.

Militants had better focus on fighting for the freedom of their minds – and soldiers, it's time to come home. It is time for conflict to be dissolved.

Forgive and forget

It is really difficult dealing with hurt feelings and heartbreak, especially if the blow was dealt from someone you loved or trusted. That sense of betrayal could easily transform into vengeance if you allow it to. Perhaps it was a spouse who said hurtful things to you, or a family member who criticised or ridiculed you; the fact that it is someone close to you makes it hurt more. A natural instinct may be to go into battle with the wrongdoer. The success of this tactic will depend on your ability, willingness and comfort level in dealing with confrontation.

> 'An eye for an eye only ends up
> making the whole world blind,'
> MAHATMA GANDHI (1869 – 1948)

Other options might be to ignore the incident, avoid dealing with it or deny the intent behind it. This does not solve the problem. Yet another option may be to distort what truly happened to make it easier for you to accept. Whatever the event, how do you forgive someone when every cell of your body detests the act and /or the person concerned? How do you bring yourself to accept, love unconditionally and forgive?

Before I share some tips, let's consider another angle. What if you were the wrongdoer? What if the pain you caused someone is eating you up inside? Worse, what if they were unaware it was you? What if you can't bring yourself to confess for fear of the consequences?

HOW TO FORGIVE YOURSELF AND OTHERS

Break the broken record. Sometimes, whether you are the wrongdoer or the aggrieved, we think about something over and over and it makes the situation worse, because time has passed, we haven't done anything about it, the awkwardness grows, the risk grows as does the fear. As the wrongdoer, find the courage to be honest and confess. Replaying the incident over and over in our minds makes it worse than it already is. As the aggrieved, however, we think that by telling the story over and over to anyone who will listen we are releasing the negative emotions around the incident. Not true. The broken record is very much what stokes the flame. It revives the pain and the hurt, keeping it very much alive. The tears may have stopped, but don't let that fool you into thinking you are 'over it,' are closer to forgiveness or being forgiven. And let's be honest, you are far from forgetting the incident by constantly talking about it! Break the broken record. Stop telling the story, stop replaying the incident and defuse the emotion. Stop punishing yourself, the wrongdoer and the poor person listening to you! And stop the exaggeration too – it may have slipped out the first few times, but any more than that then the story is no longer true, and it must stop.

If you must repeat the story, tell an empowering one. Focusing on the positives will create a different story. You will know you are telling the right story when the incident is either mentioned once in the first five seconds only, or not at all. You, as the protagonist, cannot be the victim, and the wrongdoer cannot be the villain – those stories are old-fashioned, and there is no place for such poorly crafted, self-inflicted tragedies like this in future.

For too long people have focused on the negatives, the discrimination they and others have experienced, the unfairness of life, and the atrocities of the past. Whilst I have a lot of sympathy and empathy toward the many regretted losses of our time, I have no interest in expending thought or time on the villains. I am more interested in the Phoenixes that rose from the ashes, the people who rose from adversity, the people who made a difference, the people who altered the course of life, the people who influenced destinies, the people who inspired others to their greatness. I am also interested in the people who tried. Even if they didn't fully succeed, I am encouraged by those people. They are usually the unsung heroes of our time. We need more heroes and heroines in the stories we pass onto future generations. We need people to marvel at.

What would happen if you forgave? What would happen if everyone forgot everything negative in their lives? What would life really be like then?

'The weak can never forgive. Forgiveness
is the attribute of the strong'
MAHATMA GANDHI (1869 – 1948)

Flick the switch. Understand that forgiveness is for you not for the wrongdoer. Forgiveness is a private practice. It is personal. You don't need to broadcast it to the wrongdoer or to your social circles. At the same time, if the wrongdoer seeks your forgiveness, don't withhold it. That's not kind or empowering, although it does need to be unconditional. Saying that you 'will forgive them if ...' is not forgiveness.

Forgiveness is freeing. On both sides. Forgiveness is free to give. It does not condone the wrongdoer's behaviour, nor does it exonerate them from responsibility. It simply frees you from the expectation that the past will change.

Forgiveness can be a thought, a prayer or a breath. It can be words whispered to nobody or words spoken to the wrongdoer. It could be a letter that is never sent. Whatever it is, the act of forgiving must feel like a release. It may not be possible to achieve the release instantaneously though; you may need to work on it over time. You know that you have forgiven an act or a wrongdoer when any mention of the episode or person is a non-event or you regard it with compassion.

We are all on a journey. We are all perfect for what we need to achieve in life, yet nobody is perfect. Show compassion and empathy. Recall happy memories, tell uplifting stories.

Fun: place the force of fun at the centre of what you do

Goleman talked about social skills, the importance of managing relationships and influence. I support this whole-heartedly and I believe this construct has a long way to go. People still underestimate the importance of building rapport, managing relationships, networking and maintaining healthy friendships. Furthermore, shyness, antisocial tendencies or the inability to make conversation have kept people closed off, in a bubble of perceived safety for too long. I respect and acknowledge different personalities, archetypes and social preferences. However if you are denying the essence of who you are, then I strongly believe that this has to change as the future needs all contributors to be present and accounted for. Please step forward.

My view of how we must evolve this construct is for people to place fun at the centre of their lives.

Sometimes in life we hold back, we do not engage fully in what we have, we become our own worst critics. We worry about what other people may think, we feel we don't have the time or we fool ourselves into believing going out and having fun will add to our tiredness. We also take on a mind-set of life being about sacrifice and compromise.

Absolutely not! I believe that sacrificing or compromising on something breeds resentment. If instead we operate from a place of unconditional love, abundance and acceptance then life is what is – there is no need to feel you missed out, or settled for less. Conceding prevents the feeling of fulfilment – it is only helpful for martyrs.

Happy chemicals, such as endorphins, dopamine, serotonin and oxytocin, are released in the brain when we feel good. Each of them has a role to play. The release of endorphins has been shown to increase happiness, enables people to push through pain, decreases hunger, and improves the immune response. Dopamine is the goal oriented chemical – it harbours positive stress, making you feel good, and once you have achieved something you have been working towards, the euphoria elates you, albeit temporarily. Serotonin flows when you feel significant. Oxytocin, also sometimes referred to as the cuddle hormone, is triggered when you are with someone you love and trust and you feel good. Some healthy tension between these chemicals and their related emotions, and the pressure of adrenaline and cortisol is also a good thing.

Knowing how to inject happiness into our lives and understanding the physiology around it invokes creativity and innovation in us; the joy of creating something can only be a good thing. So here are some tips on how to place fun at the centre of what you do.

HOW TO INJECT FUN INTO WHAT YOU DO

Be present – worrying about the past or future takes away the joy of the present moment. Go with the flow. Eckhart Tolle's book, *The*

Power of Now, draws on a variety of spiritual constructs, and stresses the importance of focusing on the present rather than the past or future. As he points out, you only have power over the present; you can only effect change in the present moment.

Smile. The brain releases endorphins when you smile and laugh, making you feel better. Ensure that a smile always comes across in your voice even if the person you are talking to can't see it; they need to hear it. Smileys in e-mails and on other social media convey our emotions, and are useful in clarifying our intent. Find something to smile and laugh at and about every day, a few times a day.

Find your groove. Music can help this, as does dancing, especially bad dancing if the opportunity presents itself! Do not hold back. Shake every part of your body that you are able to, for twenty minutes or more, and notice how much better you will feel.

Suspend all judgement; focus on the positives in the situation. Don't worry about looking silly. Don't judge the person who is making a fool of themselves; they are being authentic in that situation. They are making the most of the situation, and possibly even learning and creating memories from the experience of it.

Contribute to the fun at every appropriate opportunity. Work can sometimes be a serious affair – injecting some light-heartedness occasionally may not be a bad thing. Remember to have fun when playing a sport too – change the game, break the rules occasionally, make it fun for others. It's not always about winning the game, it's about making it fun for others and having fun playing it yourself.

Planning to be spontaneous is not going to work, but be spontaneous anyway! It taps into your creative side and gets the juices flowing. Create a vibe. Encourage people around you to chip in. At the end of the day, you will have fond memories and fun photos to look back on.

Laugh. That's all it takes. Laugh at something you see or hear. Or just laugh at yourself. Not taking yourself seriously definitely has to feature more in future. These are just a few examples of how to bring some fun into our already fast-paced lives.

Whilst I am a big fan of Daniel Goleman, and I encourage a way of being that demonstrates high degrees of emotional intelligence, I hope that this chapter has given you an indication of the next stage of development in emotional intelligence. There has to be greater self-belief that frees us for long enough to have fun, to focus, and to forgive. We may have neglected these attributes for a long time, so bringing it into awareness now, for the next 25 years, must surely help us achieve a shift in consciousness.

SEVEN

ENVIRONMENTAL APPRECIATION

'We're running the most dangerous experiment in history right now, which is to see how much carbon dioxide the atmosphere ... can handle before there is an environmental catastrophe.'

ELON MUSK, CEO AND CTO OF SPACEX, (BORN 1971)

Many people have excelled in spite of the environments they found themselves in. Viktor Frankl was a prime example of this: an inmate of concentration camps during the Holocaust, he wrote a book called *Man's Search for Meaning*, which continues to be a great inspiration for people defying the odds. I encourage you to read it.

I was fortunate growing up. Mum and Dad were extremely focused on ensuring that they provided everything they possibly could for us, with Dad sometimes working three jobs at a time. We lived a simple life, and worked hard at making the most of what little we had. More than just the provisions, Mum and Dad worked hard at finding opportunities that exposed us to a variety of environments necessary for our learning. Home was fun, filled with music, sports, laughter, memories and studying too. Church and charity work meant that we got to work with abandoned and sick children and people with disabilities. We were also fortunate to be exposed to 'bright lights, big city' styled environments like concerts, theatre, art exhibitions and museums, where we developed social skills, curiosity and intellect although never losing sight of our heritage and valuing family above all else.

These humble beginnings instilled in me a deep appreciation of life's treasures – peace, love and togetherness. It made me look around at the many success stories of people from disadvantaged backgrounds and how they succeeded in spite of the odds. As I looked around though, I also began noticing the deterioration of our planet's natural resources, and both the stories and the statistics inspired me to dedicate a chapter to this subject.

This chapter is aimed at three things: firstly, encouraging you to relish your current environment no matter how adverse it may seem. See the positives in it. Whether you're in a good environment, a bad environment, or that you've moved from bad to good or bad to worse, view your environment as the soil from which you will harvest one day. So, whether your environment is good or your environment is bad, your environment is great!

Secondly, look beyond the limitations of your current environment and create the environment that is conducive to the vision you have set for your life. Surround yourself with thoughts, feelings, pictures, words, colours, objects, equipment, tools, people and everything that you need to inspire you to move closer to achieving your life goals. If your circumstances prevent you from finding these items, then simply imagine them. Visualise your ideal environment with intense joy and excitement, it will create neural pathways in your brain and will spark ideas for you to explore. As you visualise, remember to take action. Dreaming provides the blueprint; action makes it reality.

And finally, with each step you take on the journey of life, actively take care of the broader environment in which you live and work: the planet – the air, the ground, the water, the trees, the animals. We can endeavour to be the best people in the world, but without a healthy planet we will perish.

How to see the positives in a negative environment

Many people find themselves in a variety of environments that are far from attractive. If you are struggling to accept or believe there are positives in your current environment, here are a few tips to help you:

- Acceptance of circumstances is the first step in making a change. Believing that circumstances are perfect (even in their imperfection) will help with acceptance.
- It may help you to temporarily or permanently remove yourself from your environment, if possible. Distance brings perspective. There is something about a change of scenery that alters thinking, forces a change in habits and therefore creates new positive habits, new interests, a new way of living. Some people are willing to change environments, but are unable to, due to circumstances outside of their control, e.g. political unrest, war. Other people are able to, but for a variety of reasons are unwilling to. If you are really passionate about and strongly believe in living your best life, and if you are able to make that move, then don't hesitate.
- Consider all the negative aspects of your environment – whether it is a dysfunctional relationship, an abusive parent, an irate boss, a rough neighbourhood, a community that has lost its way. Accept that those negative things are necessary and important factors for you to make a change. Use it as the motivation you need to achieve bigger, better, greater outcomes. Find reasons why all the bad elements of your environment are a good thing. Write a list. If you are struggling with this, ask someone for help. Do a role play. A different perspective may be helpful in changing your association with the environment you have come from.
- Adopt a mind-set of positivity. Believe that everything has a

higher meaning and that it is contributing to you achieving your life purpose. This is important in maintaining focus on the true goal.

How to create an environment conducive to your life vision

Here are a few examples of things you can do to create the ideal environment in which your vision can be realised:

- Surround yourself with what will enable you to achieve your vision: books, people, music, art, sports, or items representing the vision. If you are envisaging a high profile business career for yourself in future, be that person in that role right now, behave like it, become it. Surround yourself with people and artefacts that go with that environment. Speak to people who are already in this environment. Ask them to describe their experiences; imagine that you are part of that too. Surround yourself with pictures of the environment you want to create. Use your vision board for this perhaps.

- Remove the distractions in your current environment or thought sphere that do not serve your life vision: unhelpful television programmes, gossip magazines, games, or negative people. These aspects dilute enthusiasm toward working toward your goal, remove focus and result in you losing momentum.

'Be a yardstick of quality. Some people aren't used to an environment where excellence is expected,'
STEVE JOBS (1955 – 2011)

There has to be alignment. Purpose, direction, commitment.

How to preserve the environment

It has become a planetary emergency and we must all contribute to the solution for preserving the environment. It is no longer just about governments, big companies and environmental campaigners. It's about the mind-set that goes with littering in public places, illegal dumping of waste, not doing household recycling, creating CO_2 emissions, industrial waste disposal, preservation of the forests, and conservation of wildlife. There is plenty of information about how to look after the planet and its resources, where to invest in sustainable and alternative energy, what the developments in bio fuels are, and how you can actually save and make money from implementing these initiatives that benefit the planet. Yet we remain in the predicament we are in today with a suffering planet. What will it take for us to collectively make a seismic shift on how we treat the planet?

Whilst the environmental advocates mentioned in Chapter One (Rachel Carson, David Attenborough, Al Gore), together with other awareness campaigns, have effected a positive change in how we preserve the planet, it is sadly not enough to make the shift that is needed. Sustainable energy provision and waste disposal remain a top priority.

There is a huge global movement for households, business and industrial organisations to minimise waste. The primary aim is waste reduction at source followed by reuse, recycling, treatment and appropriate safe disposal. New initiatives are exploring how to convert waste into bio-fuels, while others attempt to reduce the amount of waste going to landfill sites, implementing extensive recycling programmes ranging from kerbside collections to public recycling centres and bottle banks, as well as developing other reduce, reuse, and recycle programmes. In many countries littering, including pet fouling, is considered antisocial behaviour, and is liable for a penalty.

Water conservation has also become a necessity in recent years, with various campaigners, governments and schools promoting rain harvesting, encouraging communities to report water leakages to local authorities as soon as possible and environmental agencies joining forces with businesses to protect waters from pollution.

Other areas of focus include the reduction in CO_2 emissions. Encouraging the use of bicycles in inner cities is increasing in popularity. Ken Livingstone, then Mayor of London, announced in 2008 that he wished to trial a public bicycle hire scheme like the Vélib network in Paris to encourage people to use bicycles within the city for short journeys, thereby helping reduce carbon emissions. The initiative was implemented by Boris Johnson in 2010, and 'Boris Bikes' have been a huge success since then in London.

In addition to these initiatives, businesses are also playing a major role in environmental sustainability measures. Companies like Capgemini adopt a 'follow-me' printer service, where a document is sent to a printer but it only prints once you scan your security pass at the printer. This eliminates any wastage of printing not being collected, and print jobs being forgotten, discarded or carried away accidentally by colleagues.

Other initiatives across industry include things like using alternative energy sources e.g. solar powered panels to power geysers, swimming pools and other household appliances are increasing in popularity and reducing in cost as regular improvements are being made. Germany reported having supplied as much as 50% of its power through solar power during parts of June 2014.

Back in the mid-2000s, many of the major banks implemented credit cards whose rewards included more than just the usual air miles and discounts on groceries. Each purchase resulted in a contribution to a charity or environmental project. The Barclaycard itself was made from biodegradable material. Finextra (2008) reported that Rabobank's Climate Credit Card, from 2006 onwards, calculated consumers' carbon emissions based on their purchases and offset it with carbon credits.

The introduction of the Kyoto Protocol, linked to the United Nations Framework Convention on Climate Change (UNFCCC), placed binding obligations on countries to reduce high emissions. The European Union's Emissions Trading Scheme (EU ETS) was introduced in January 2005 to facilitate the trading of industrialised countries' emissions reduction commitments under the Kyoto Protocol. Financial institutions such as Barclays Capital, Deutsche Bank and others set up trading desks soon after its introduction. *'When one considers that the emissions market is now worth $30 billion and is predicted to grow to $1 trillion in the next decade,'* says Sarah McGeachie and Sarah Parkinson of PricewaterhouseCoopers Canada (2008), *'being prepared to take advantage of such market growth is a compelling argument.'*

In addition to banking initiatives, the United Nations Environment Programme (UNEP) has highlighted several ways of increasing the awareness of environmental issues worldwide.

Communications and education programmes such as environmental awareness campaigns were considered most successful when targeted at specific groups. From my experience of managing change programmes, where behavioural change interventions were critical in making change stick, regular communications that took people on a journey, whilst describing the actual impact and consequences of their choices was a powerful way of getting people to change their habits. And as we work our way into the future, more of this needs to be done.

The power of mass media goes a long way in creating awareness, educating and instigating change. In developed countries and urban areas, the use of print, broadcast, and Internet media can be a great way to increase education and awareness.

Local environmental education campaigns are just as important in the developing world as in industrialised nations. However, reaching out to the people in those countries can be difficult due to language barriers, illiteracy, and cultural differences.

Awareness campaigns delivered in classroom settings is another way of building awareness from a young age. According to UNEP, thirty percent of the world's population is under the age of 18, so educating children and young adults about environmental problems this early on will be crucial to long-term success.

We are out of time.

If you live in countries where recycling is not mandated by your local authority, be proactive: change your household waste disposal practices and start recycling today. In Johannesburg, for example, there are recycling bins available at most service stations for you to place your recyclable items into, while private companies are now providing recycling services for a small fee. Recycling is simpler than you may think: separate paper, plastics, glass and tin cans. Raw food waste can form organic compost for your garden. Install a water tank, or two or three or more, to collect rain water. Put pressure on local businesses to adopt environmentally friendly practices. Insist on corporates seriously adhering to their corporate sustainability policies. Better still, if you are inside a local business or large corporate, encourage them to revisit their policies and business practices. Blowing the whistle on them like Erin Brockovich did is not ideal, but necessary if they are not taking heed and are continuing to damage the environment, and wellbeing of communities.

EIGHT

EXERCISE TO ENERGISE

'Training gives us an outlet for suppressed energies
created by stress and thus tones the spirit just
as exercise conditions the body.'

ARNOLD SCHWARZENEGGER

The pace of change over the last 25 years has been exponential. If that trajectory continues, or steepens, it can only mean that the next 25 years is going to be even more demanding. We will be expected to work harder, think faster, make better decisions, be on call for longer. If we're finding the pace today demanding, how will we cope with the demands of the future at triple the speed?

I may disappoint some of you with this chapter: it does not advocate the latest, hottest exercise programme, nor does it evaluate the current diets taking the world by storm. If you're hoping it is going to criticise caramel and condone cauliflower, or the other way around, it's not. I will provide you with only as much fact as will bring tears to your eyes.

- You need to exercise; you know this already – stop messing about, get on with it.
- You need to eat healthy food in small quantities; you know this already – stop messing about, get on with it.
- You need to drink water in large quantities; you know this already – stop messing about, get on with it.
- You need to sleep for seven hours a night to function optimally.
- You need to remove the toxins: quit smoking, moderate your alcohol intake and give up popping those non-essential pills.

There is no question that the mind is powerful. However, all the thinking and visualising of yourself exercising will not achieve the result of actually exercising. All thought requires action to deliver results. I hope that reading this will cause a shift in how you relate to food and exercise; that you will exercise the way you want to because you will also derive pleasure from it. I hope that you will be inspired to consume the right quantities and best types of food that fuel your body to live your passion.

The magic is simply about you making a decision to exercise your brain to energise your body and your mind. Choose before it is chosen for you.

I remember that fateful day clearly. The day my life changed, and with it my mind-set toward many aspects of life. All I did was reach for a cup. Well, not really, as I later discovered.

Looking back on it now, it reminds me of an episode of the US TV series *24*. In 24 hours the decision to take my body (and my life) seriously was made for me. I was rooted to the spot on the platform of Tottenham Court Road Station on the London Underground. Hundreds of people bustled around me, jostling because I really shouldn't have been standing in the middle of the platform during what was clearly peak time. I tried to make sense of the signage on the wall. Was I waiting to board a Central Line train to go home, or had I stepped off the Central Line to connect to the Northern Line to get to my client? I seemed to have forgotten. The platform was underground, so judging the time based on daylight was not an option. I looked at the station clock hoping it would tell me – its analogue needles pointed to 6:25. I couldn't work out whether it was morning or evening. I knew though that it was a cold weekday – my work suit buried under a warm woollen coat, scarf and gloves, told me that much. I couldn't make sense of the suitcase I had with me though. That was not the priority at the moment. Rather, the time was bothering me.

Moving out of the way, I laughed at myself, thinking how silly of me to not know where I was going. I just needed a minute to get my bearings. The next train arrived at the platform with a gust of icy wind, but unfortunately the knowing did not come with it. The decision about what to do next did not appear with the train that followed that one either. Panic started to rise. I tried to think about the last hour. Blank. I tried to recall whom I'd seen, what I'd eaten, where I'd been. Blank. My only memory was standing on the platform. I sat down on the platform bench feeling confused. Having a suitcase added to the complexity of sorting through my memory. Someone sat next to me. I looked over. He avoided my stare. That's acceptable practice in London. I leaned over. He leaned away. That's normal too in London. I knew I had to find my words. A train came. The man left. More people. Came. Left. More noise. More wind. It was getting colder. Night or day, I still didn't know, but it was getting late either way. My panic rose. I searched all my senses to give me a clue on what to do. Adrenaline stood no chance against the numbness in my body. My eyes were working fine; hands, feet and mouth frozen. It felt like a partial stroke, a semi brain freeze and half a breakdown all at once. Thoughts were spinning but no movement was possible.

Fast forward to today: I am sitting in my office, soft classical music in the background, a delicious cup of coffee steaming up the nearby magical window which I look out of for inspiration as I write. The pool glistens in the sunlight, the dogs tumble playfully over each other in the garden as beautiful birds in a spectrum of colours try to pick on the seeds I've thrown earlier. Bliss. So different to where I was then.

So what exactly happened that day? That day was the end of a period of madness. Strategically important clients, I was leading several projects, large teams of consultants on business critical projects, facing off to senior leaders, with deadlines pulled forward and co-ordinated sleep shifts with various team members. I was flying across different time zones for major international events, on planes and trains and taxis, with heavy bags – lifting, running, wheeling, carrying. The pace was crazy – three reports were due that week alone, including huge volumes of data to analyse. I had been working 21-hour days, 7-day weeks, barely time to go to the loo, no time to eat, far too much extra sweet coffee to compensate, no daylight, no exercise, no nutrition, no life. Now multiply that by 18 months.

My body had been screaming 'Stop!' at me for the longest time, but I hadn't listened. I kept pushing, working off adrenaline. I was on this hamster wheel, going round and round, faster and faster, except I had lost sight of where I was going, and most importantly why I was on this hamster wheel. Somehow I'd also created a few hamster wheels to prove something ridiculous to myself – that I can do it all. I would have kept going, I guess, fooled into believing I was 'fulfilled by the variety it brought to my life' but the Universe was kind to me, I realised later, and dealt me a blow that scared me enough to take action that day.

Attempts to connect with anybody on the platform that day failed. Everybody was too rushed, and I was not making sense. I somehow managed to make my way up to the street level. I remember distinctly crumpling to the floor, overwhelmed by the relief of knowing that it was night time, that I wouldn't have to go to work now, to endure another 20 hours of work feeling the way I did. I noticed a pub nearby, with people happily singing and toasting other colleagues. I should have been having fun too. Instead I was in pain, and something major had happened, but I couldn't remember what it was. I felt crushed and empty at the same time. What had happened? It was something big, but I just couldn't remember. The suitcase had something to do with it. Where had I come from? Or was I going somewhere? I was worn out. I grappled for my phone. I needed to call Shakeer. My phone was dead.

I managed to hail a cab. The luggage tag on my suitcase reminded me of where I lived. The cab driver kept looking at me in the rear view mirror as he drove me home, probably wondering if I was ill, and hoping that I wouldn't throw up in the cab. Strangely, I got home just before midnight. I don't know where the time went. I collapsed into bed next to Shakeer, who sleepily rubbed my head and said, 'You're home early this week, that's nice!' He was right, a pre-midnight arrival was unusual!

The next morning I was up first, showered, changed, headed to the kitchen to grab a coffee before I left. I passed that suitcase again in the hallway. I stared at it curiously as I filled the kettle with water. I still couldn't figure how it fit into the jigsaw puzzle. The events of the last few days were still a blur. Jazzy and Lucy lazily pattered about keeping me company in the kitchen. And then it happened.

All I did was reach for a cup – and an almighty pain shot up my spine, immobilising me completely. The pain was excruciating. I cried out, but the pain choked my voice away. My vision blurred. I began to feel dizzy. As I hit the floor, I managed to say to Jazzy, 'Find Dad', a game that we played often, and I knew he would respond to, inadvertently getting help. Just before I passed out, I saw the suitcase again, and the hallway clock just above it showed 6:25.

Days later, I was at the hospital, waiting for the neurosurgeon to give me the all-clear. When he finally came in, he showed me the MRI scans and the X-rays, but I couldn't quite hear or understand him properly, maybe it was the anaesthetic, or the exhaustion or both, or maybe I was just in denial. It had something to do with disc degeneration, and scoliosis he seemed to say, as well as my sacroiliac joint – the sacrum which supports the spine and the ilium bone in the pelvic area. Something complicated ... then something else... Then another something happened which caused a slight shift with the bones, causing the immobility, inflammation and excruciating pain. He spoke for a long time describing in detail what had happened. It wasn't reaching for the cup that did it. It was my harsh treatment of my body that had led to this result. Bad posture, lifting heavy suitcases, running for trains and planes, wearing uncomfortable shoes, stretching and bending incorrectly, not eating nourishing food, not resting properly. Basically the perfect recipe to break my back, so to speak. The good news, though, was that I would regain full body movement within two years. That's all I needed to know. That was my moment of clarity. My future lay right here. I was given crutches and a back brace, and had to endure months of physiotherapy.

For the first few weeks, I could not get into a sitting, standing or lying down position unaided. Shakeer had to build a lot of muscle and patience to help me. Most days he virtually carried me around – getting up and down stairs was the worst. At night, I would wake him up several times to turn me on my side, or help me back onto my back, or turn me to the other side. As a result, most nights were sleepless nights for us both, me in pain, him feeling helpless. I was cooped up for the most part in the house, and I hated it. It agitated me. My only outing in the beginning was physiotherapy. It was awful. I found myself becoming stressed as it approached each week. Physiotherapy meant trying and eliminating things that did not improve my mobility. Things that did not work were discovered through excruciating pain.

In time I began to feel better. It took ages to get to this point, but eventually I was well enough to return to work. I was really looking forward to getting out the house. I was only at 60% full capacity, but the company that I worked for were wonderfully accommodating, making every effort to get me back to full capacity. I had to make some drastic changes. Pretty much everything about what I did and how I did it needed to change. I had to dress differently – my back brace was relatively 'eye-catching' so I wore bulky clothes to hide it – somehow I felt worse. I had to wear flat shoes that were rather unflattering to maintain balance and stabilise my gait. As if that wasn't enough, who would have thought that re-evaluating my 'bags strategy' would form part of my recuperation plan, but it did. It was clear that the suitcase needed to be packed away for a while … and there was something about that suitcase that I still needed closure on, but I will have to get to that later.

Next on the list: my handbags needed to be downsized. I could no longer carry anything big or heavy, so petite little handbags became the order of the day. Taking my laptop everywhere I went was also no longer an option. No more heavy back-packs, or carrying files and documents that I may need for the odd meeting; I now had to be super-organised with what I needed when. Even with this adjustment, it took me 4 times as long to get anywhere and I was in constant agony. Pain killers and anti-inflammatory medication temporarily eased the suffering but with it came the dulling of my energy levels and concentration too. I pushed on at work, I was a trooper, but I was slowly sinking into a negative state without realising it. Soon I began questioning everything I was doing. I became restless. Something was missing. I realised rather suddenly it was time for a change of environment.

Thank Goodness, Christmas and New Year were around the corner, and some festive time off work would be welcome. I used this time constructively, spending time with people who mattered. Able to stand and get around better after months of physiotherapy, meant that I could cook us a proper meal for the first time in a long time and this time we even ate home-cooked vegetables! Our closest friends, who were really our family away from home, were there that cold wintry Christmas Eve as the fireplace crackled. I remembered Tottenham Court Road Station Platform. I remembered where I had flown in from earlier that day. It was then that I announced my life changing decision to my friends: to quit my 6-figure paying job, 'become an entrepreneur' and move to South Africa.

For the first few months as I waited for the shipment of our cars, furniture and personal possessions to arrive, there was little I could do but continue the rest and recovery journey that I had been on for over a year, following my back injury. The change of environment brought remarkable perspective. There was no messing about. I had to get serious about my recovery. There was no logical or legitimate answer to the question of why had I not looked after my body.

Alongside recuperating in South Africa, I needed something to stimulate my mind. My business kicked off nicely. I loved every minute of it, because I was doing purpose-driven work. I worked on important projects, with amazing people. I could see immediate results. It energised me. We were achieving life-altering feats in accelerated timescales.

I exercise more in a day than I used to in a year. Despite the long days I still have time to cook, and practice makes perfect, well for ten dishes anyway! I spend quality time with my family and take the dogs for a walk in the park a few times a week. I found my sense of humour again. My back is 90% recovered. The bills are getting paid. I live in a crime-ridden and violent city yet I thrive on the blend of optimism and hopelessness that surrounds me, because it gives me an environment in which to do work that makes a difference – one person at a time, one initiative at a time. I am constantly in a good mood and I work with others to help them find the same. I have more energy than I have ever had. I love my life. How is this possible? What happened?

A few things happened.

Firstly I reached my 'tipping point', the point at which circumstances brought me to take a serious look at my life, which I have yet to share with you in the following chapters. It created that paralysis in me at Tottenham Court Road station that night. Intellectually, I knew that my life had gone off-track slightly, yet for years I denied it and continued on the same path until my body quietened my head for long enough to hear the voice of my soul get me back on track.

Next, whatever life-altering decision I made, I knew it had to be supported by a shift in mind-set – so I pretended this new phase of life will be my 'retirement'; that this is how my life is going to be until I leave the planet, whether that's tomorrow or by 2040, beyond or between. This has remarkably shaped every choice I have made on what to take on and where to focus. Living as if every day is my last is deeply rewarding. Now, I know it would have more impact if I was actually dying as I say this, but here's the irony: I was dying when I wasn't doing the right things. My soul was withering away from the lack of purpose, my brain from the lack of stimulation and my body from the lack of nourishment.

And even though I am describing my personal journey here, I believe much of what I am going to say will be something you can relate to and will hopefully inspire you to make a change, not just for now, but for your future too.

My body had been neglected for a long time. Too much caffeine and sugar, too few nutrients. As someone who does not believe in diets, I resorted to a few simple changes that had a huge impact. Firstly, I cut down coffee to just one cup a day; I cut out hot chocolate completely in winter months; and I drink up to two litres of water a day, which became easier to drink in a warm climate. I became a vegetarian and cut out bread entirely for one year. Green leafy vegetables and dried fruit supplied my body's iron needs, while pasta, porridge and pulses supplied the energy my brain and body needed, as they release glucose slowly and steadily. It was amazing. I wasn't even trying but I shed all the excess weight without doing anything, and bizarrely I dropped a whole shoe size and a half! I felt more energetic and, interestingly I didn't need so much sleep. Over time and in a very natural way I reintroduced fish and chicken to my diet. I made a conscious effort to ensure that fresh vegetables featured at least 3 days per week in my food plan, despite the fact that I am a very bad vegetable cook. Thank goodness for my sisters, mum and aunt, who are very sympathetic and help me out in that area. Fruit, juices, soups and salads are easier during their respective seasons. For example, as someone who doesn't cope well with the cold I often went through winter on stodge. No fruit, juices or salads at all for the nine months that winter lasted in the UK. Easy. Not good.

Now that I am in South Africa I have found a way to have balanced meals – smaller quantities of healthy food. I deny myself nothing. Despite the warnings I eat cheese every day. I started when I was four and I will stop when my body tells me to. I allow myself to binge occasionally. Inevitably, I believe that my body lacks what it needs at the time but will regulate itself. I listen to my body. I have seen a marked improvement in my brain function. I realised that the neurotransmitters in my brain were not getting the protein that they needed from my diet to function optimally and since adjusting my diet, I have noticed the benefits of improved recollection and faster numeric calculations. Radically reducing my carbohydrate intake prevented the sugar rushes followed by the late afternoon lows. The 'steadiness' it gave me was priceless.

I love music. So I make a concerted effort to listen to my favourite music tracks every day, reserving special tracks for certain occasions. I play the *Rocky* movie soundtrack, for example, on repeat before every major event, meeting, seminar, presentation, coaching session, training course or consulting workshop. The movie is my favourite of all time. I crank up the volume on my iPod – listening to upbeat music heightens my mental agility. It helps me get to my peak performance state and I think and function at my best. It's not possible for me to help people achieve breakthroughs in their lives if I am not firing on all cylinders – it wouldn't be fair. Music nourishes my soul.

I renamed exercise – which felt like a scary, demanding word; a chore. I wanted something more pleasurable. So instead I go for 'leisurely strolls' or 'I run with the dogs' or I 'play' the hoover, or I make the car 'look beautiful' and 'create a sparkling floor'. I started small with this task. And it worked. The endorphins helped – blocking out the pain, minimising the discomfort of the exercise and providing feelings of euphoria once I had achieved my exercise goal for the day. Now I have committed to an hour of movement every day, as Gretchen Reynolds, in her book, *The First 20 minutes,* says, '*The first 20 minutes of moving around, if someone has been really sedentary, provide most of the health benefits. You get prolonged life, reduced disease risk — all of those things come in in the first 20 minutes of being active.*'

For me that means slow jogging, brisk walking, scrubbing, washing, but it's always a full body workout – my heart rate goes up and I break a sweat. Most importantly, I approach it with fun; I realised I need both fun and a challenge to stay interested in exercise. I noticed small but important changes: walking up stairs became easier – I was no longer out of breath or wheezy; I had more energy; I was in a better mood; and I remembered things better.

In addition to exercising and nourishing my body, I exercised and nourished my brain. It's amazing how much you can do with less sleep and more energy. I did a little bit of everything that stretched me intellectually, emotionally, creatively, but in ways that were different to my consulting profession. I played Sudoku, did more crossword puzzles and downloaded a few more apps that trained my brain to be sharper. I tutored people on various subjects as I came across them. I read for pleasure. Crime, thrillers and, much to my husband's dismay, a few romance novels too. I've always had a love for writing, so when I applied to be a regular columnist for the *International Coaching News* magazine and the CEO instead offered that I run the magazine, it was hard to say that it was a dream come true because I had never dreamed that big. Needless to say, I jumped at the opportunity. Running the magazine has been fantastic. I got to work with many international authors, academics and specialists in business, coaching and leadership.

My attempts to learn a new language failed dismally, but undeterred I decided to learn five key phrases in three of my favourite languages. Also, inspired by my father's artistry, I asked him to help me refresh my drawing skills. After a few weeks, he bought me a book on how to draw cartoons and stopped giving me art lessons. I guess he was right, it was definitely easier on my ego to be laughed at this way!

I changed how I respond to stressful situations. I regard stress as a simple mismatch between my expectation and reality. No need for unnecessary emotion anymore. I use *motion* instead to dissolve stress if it occurs. For example, I walk around my office when I have stressful or conflict-ridden telephone conversations. I have standing up meetings where possible, drawing on some research which shows we have 7% more brain activity when standing. I get more oxygen to my brain through movement, through mindful breathing, through awareness; and I am able to produce better quality thoughts and ideas as a result. I promised myself that everything I did had to be enjoyable. Much of what I did was *not* enjoyable in the early days of moving back to South Africa, but I persevered and found a way every single time to find pleasure or reward in everything I did. I reframed my perception of the tasks that I was avoiding, I interacted warmly with people who were cold and nasty, and I stayed longer at the places I wanted to run away from.

That being said, I had to get real with myself. It's not all warm and snug or cool and rosy. Life's tough. I was human. I needed to interact with life differently, not just to cope better, but to exercise my brain and energise my body, rather than be bogged down by circumstance. So I always spoke my mind. I was always professional and dignified. I had to learn the language for this. It is hard to change speech patterns. I showed empathy and compassion. My intentions were pure, even if my words sounded harsh in the early days. This made a huge difference. I connected with so many precious people, but had to make tough choices and distance myself from negative people too.

I joined a few networking and interest groups. The life of a 'retired' entrepreneur was a lonely one. Moving back to South Africa after 12 years meant that I had lost my personal and professional networks. I wanted to meet people, have a chat, laugh, share ideas, go to new places, expand my horizons. Connecting with people certainly put my life, purpose and priorities into perspective, and strengthened my resolve. Most times, as I do small bits of charity work, my emotions seesaw between extreme sadness at the plight of people, animals and the environment, and severe anger at the apathy and harmful actions of people, business and governments. I get through it by ensuring that I make a difference to someone or something every day – whether it's a friend, colleague, stranger, animal, it doesn't matter, but each day needs to count for something.

I decided to teach. The part rebel and part insecure little girl in me resisted it for long enough, but it was time. Anyone who wanted to learn something that I could impart, they asked and I would teach. I also signed up to lecture and coach at local universities. This is incredibly rewarding. I am so glad that I was open to exploring new paths, otherwise I would have missed out on one of the most energising activities in life, to learn through teaching. Besides, how else do I role model the philosophy of 'face your fears'?

Changing my environment was necessary for me to support this shift in my life. For some reason, being a retired entrepreneur in the middle of London was incomprehensible for me. Yet in South Africa it was almost a given. I was compelled to build new infrastructure, which in turn built my commitment to the cause I was pursuing.

And finally, I meditate often. Quietening my mind does wonders. I also rest often. And I would encourage you to do the same, especially if you are studying or taking tests the next day. Researchers from Brown University have shown that the brain consolidates learning better during the four sleep stages because more energy is available and there are fewer distractions. Each sleep stage is associated with different brainwaves which connect to different parts of the brain, depending on what has been learnt. Other studies show that test results are better after a good night's sleep. When we first moved back to South Africa, I slept a lot. My family teased that as I'd arrived at the start of Autumn, I was going into hibernation. Daytime temperatures of 24° Celsius and pouring sunlight continuously for eleven months was hardly winter, but they were right, I was hibernating; cocooning, almost; rejuvenating my mind and body;

renewing myself. I did it without any feelings of guilt or anxiety. My body and my mind needed it; I felt all the better for it and everyone I work with now reaps the rewards of me being at the top of my game. Now that I'm over the hump of exhaustion and my back is almost fully recovered, my favourite past time is daydreaming in the garden or at the poolside. Some of my greatest realisations happen right there. Acting on those realisations is what brought me here today.

Now I realise this lifestyle may sound like a dream, especially if you're a single mum, or working a few jobs to make ends meet, or you've been out of work for a long time. You're already feeling exhausted, frustrated and anxious. You feel like you don't have the energy to move. One more thing will break the proverbial camel's back, no matter how small. I am sharing this with you in the hope that you will relate to it on a personal level. I want you to know you can live the life of your dreams and still make a difference to the planet and our future, because even though I described how leisurely my life is, actually leisure time constitutes only two hours of my day! I made it seem and sound like it was longer than that, but that is because I shifted my association with time. Could you do the same?

Shifting my association with time has been life-changing. The time that I have is short, but the value I place on it is huge. What you read was my perceived value from limited time, which is exponentially greater than just time itself. You can do the same. What you do with the time that you have is more important than time itself.

Inside your brain lies a gem of infinite magic. You've perhaps been too busy or maybe didn't need to activate it until now. Now is your time. Your coping mechanisms are stretched to the limit, you cannot go on like this for much longer. Activation is a simple process of concentrating on this magical gem in your brain and believing that it is there. It will provide you with all that you need when you are ready.

So get ready fast. It has the power to provide you with energy when you are tired, joy when you are anxious, peace when you are troubled. I also believe you can heal your own illnesses and diseases through the power of the brain. If what you have contracted is something that has come up as a result of your lifestyle, you really can overcome it. I know this because it has been done thousands of times over, and if it's been done once, it can be done again. You just need to choose to want to do it.

Research has shown that increasing physical activity improves the blood and oxygen flow to the brain. This promotes the production of new cells and neural connections which stimulate the production of endorphins, which in turn reduce stress levels.

Harvard psychiatrist Dr John Ratey explains this concept in his book, *Spark: The Revolutionary New Science of Exercise and the Brain*. He outlines how exercise stimulates brain cells, readying them to learn. This in turn results in the production of a chemical called the brain-derived neurotropic factor (BNDF), which amongst other things improves memory. *'It's like Miracle-Gro for the brain,' he says. 'About 30 minutes of moderate aerobic activity (brisk walking, swimming, vigorous yard work), five days a week is required to create enough BNDF to keep your mind sharp with age.'*

Exercise improves health at all ages. It is never too late to start exercising. Increasing cardio-vascular health radically reduces the risk of heart attacks and strokes. Studies have consistently provided evidence that exercise reduces the rate of cognitive decline in older adults and delays the onset of dementia due to Alzheimer's disease. Exercise can boost cognitive function in adults with mild cognitive impairment who are in the early stages of Alzheimer's and at high risk of progressing to dementia. More than 40 million people in the US are over the age of 65, and this number is expected to double by 2040.

'Age related mental impairment rates increase from 10 percent among 70-year olds to as much as 40 percent in 85-year olds,' claimed

the Brain Research Foundation survey in 2013. *'In a six year study of more than 1,700 people age 65 and older, researchers at the University of Washington in Tacoma found that those who exercised three times a week had a 32 percent lower risk of dementia than those who were sedentary,'* said Dr Greg Wells in the *Globe and Mail*, (May 2014).

Another study by researchers at the University of Illinois at Urbana-Champaign found that as little as 20 minutes of yoga can help improve brain power. *'It appears that following yoga practice, the participants were better able to focus their mental resources, process information quickly, more accurately and also learn, hold and update pieces of information more effectively than after performing a bout of aerobic exercise,'* lead author Neha Gothe said, according to PsyBlog.

A study done in Illinois revealed that where schools implemented a programme of aerobic exercise, they found a direct correlation between fitness and academic performance, where as little as 20 minutes of walking before a test can raise a child's test scores. Their study found that exercise stimulates the 'feel good' neurotransmitters in the brain. One of their case studies, a school in Missouri plagued with frequent violence, found that their discipline problems decreased by two-thirds after starting a daily exercise programme for students.

So here's an opportunity. Take control of your mind. Command it to serve you in ways that best help you achieve your divine purpose. Focus on what you want. If it's a healthier body then define what a healthy body means for you. Be realistic. Now get your mind to help your body achieve this. If it's a better eating plan, again write down what that means for you and declare it out loud. Better still, focus on what outcome eating a certain way will deliver for you. Remember, food creates fuel for the body – if the body is fuelled, where do you want to take it? What results do you want to achieve?

Change your thinking. Just like that. Make a decision right now on how you would like your life to be. It doesn't matter what the masses are saying or doing or what the genetic disposition of your family may be. Just do it, as Nike famously says. If you can do it once it can be repeated. A good example of a great feat done once and then repeated, was the men's 100 metre race. The race had never breached 10 seconds during the 72 years that it had been run since 1896, until on one night in Sacramento, 20th June 1968, the 'Night of Speed', three men ran it in under 10 seconds. Jim Hines, Ronnie Ray Smith and Charles Greene were the first to break the 10-second barrier in the 100 metre sprint. With every decade that followed an increasing number of athletes ran in under 10 seconds, culminating in seven of the eight finalists running less than 10 seconds during the 2012 Men's 100 metre Olympic final in London.

Just believing that a feat can be achieved is most of the battle in energising your body and mind. Go for it! Live your greatness.

NINE

ENROLMENT CREATES ECHOES IN THE WORLD

'The key is to keep company only with people who uplift you, whose presence calls forth your best,'
EPICTETUS, GREEK SAGE & PHILOSOPHER (AD C. 55 – 135)

In a world that is becoming faster, fuller and more competitive, and even though we are more connected through social media, our success will be dependent on greater levels of collaboration than before. We will need to move away from working in siloes and encourage greater co-operation to develop innovative solutions that address the looming business, environmental and life challenges lying ahead.

Enrolment for me is the act of engaging people in your vision. I want to extrapolate on this definition: as you exude your passions in all you do, live your higher purpose and serve others, people will gravitate toward you, will want to stand by you and will automatically enrol in what you stand for. Personal choice secures the greatest level of commitment. And a greater number of people working on something make for a more sustainable solution. This is a fundamental construct of the future.

'If your actions inspire others to dream more, learn more, do more and become more, you are a leader,'

JOHN QUINCY ADAMS, AMERICAN STATESMAN (1767 – 1848)

Enrolment is not about the ego, popularity or creating a fan base. It is not about enticing people to your cause. It is not a following or a cult. It is not about convincing or influencing. It is about your authenticity and displaying integrity in all you do. The elasticity of your vision attracts people. Your expansive nature attracts people to you to help you fulfil a purpose. As for this term 'echoes' and its importance – well, more people energised and excited and talking about what you are collectively working on, facilitates a transformation in the world. Each of you becomes a role model, an exemplar in your sphere of influence. Families grow, communities grow. A critical mass is created. Your echo engages others. It reverberates. Shared values become an underlying factor to achieving success. And very soon your echoes become sonic booms.

If you are thinking that you are not quite the leader, market maker or centre of gravity, that's okay. If, however, you are looking around to latch onto someone else's cause as a means to fulfilling an empty space in yourself, it may be a good learning opportunity for you temporarily, but it will not be sustainable for you in the long run. If, during that process, however, you uncover something in you that is being fulfilled, then time spent there will certainly have been worthwhile. I am not referring to fame on the world stage – simply being a super mum or dad, a good neighbour or friend, or a helpful work colleague is enough. My only ask is that you be the best version of yourself at all times.

Find something that interests you so when the opportunity arises you will notice it. Apply the entrepreneurial wisdom described earlier and if, after undertaking all the due diligence, you still feel it is something worth pursuing, then go for it. It may be a new business idea or taking up a new hobby. You don't need to be centre stage to lead; you don't need to lead in all aspects of your life. You could lead from the front as a parent, and you could lead from within in your career or from within your community. Many of the world's top leaders lead from within. They are not exactly heralded in the media but they are often the people who really get things done. They're the unsung heroes. Our world would not be the same without them. Be a role model – there is success in that too. Do it with charm, compassion and authenticity.

Enrolment achieves change, and change can only happen if there's a critical mass. A critical mass is defined *'as a sufficient number of adopters of an innovation so that the rate of adoption becomes self-sustaining and creates further growth'*. It is an aspect of the theory of 'Diffusion of Innovations', where Everett Rogers, talks of mass market acceptance occurring at between 15-18% penetration which causes a tipping point. He says that 2.5% are innovators, 13.5% are early adopters, 34% become the early majority, a further 34% follow and become the late majority, followed by the last 16% who are the 'laggers'.

Building a critical mass starts with one person and a great idea. This concept however got me wondering: how do you allow yourself to believe in this great idea?

For some people there are small adjustments to be made; for others this may mean a life transformation. Some people are burdened with procrastination. They know full well something must be done, but finding the oomph or the '*vooma*' (lovely South African word) to get up, do something or make that change, is difficult to muster. Some people are blessed with just knowing their destiny, while the rest of us either bumble along or stumble upon it one day without even realising. Some have a light-bulb moment, a flick of a switch in their hearts or minds, a turning point – people call it different things – but it is a definitive moment where a path changes and a decision is made.

Malcolm Gladwell coined the phrase 'tipping point'. He argues that many problems, from crime to teenage delinquency and traffic jams, behave like epidemics that are capable of sudden and dramatic changes in direction; yet the right intervention at just the right time – the tipping point – can start a cascade of change and provide a method for developing strategies for everything from raising a child to running a company.

With this in mind, I spent several months researching the conditions under which people connected with their life purpose, or made strategically important, life changing decisions, which left them completely fulfilled.

My hope is that this decision-making model will enable you to understand more about what causes people to make life-changing decisions, and how enrolment can only be possible during moments of decision.

Whether you are stuck, feel like you are a victim of circumstance or fate, or feel inspired to change and don't know how, this model could help. It is not going to help you make that decision, or get people enrolled in what you stand for, but it talks to the conditions that need to be in place for decisions to be made and for enrolment to be successful. Once that decision is made you embark on a life path where thoughts, words and actions are completely aligned to your values and life purpose, and enrolment of others into your vision becomes a natural unfolding of your collective vision into reality.

My research explored the conditions under which instantaneous change is made with no regret, no doubt and no delay. It was extensive: academic texts, internet based content from leading thinkers and interviews with people who believed they had made life changing decisions. In the end I concluded that there are three triggers to a life-changing decision:

1. Feeling a deep emotional connection to something that triggered a feeling of 'I must do xyz'. This taps into a deep human condition and drives you toward a positive goal.
2. Having an experience which breaches your tolerance threshold, triggering a feeling of, 'I've had enough!' This compels you to move away from negative circumstances.
3. Experiencing a radical change in circumstances, usually something that is out of your control, which leaves you feeling like, 'I have no choice'. This forces you to create something new for yourself to work towards.

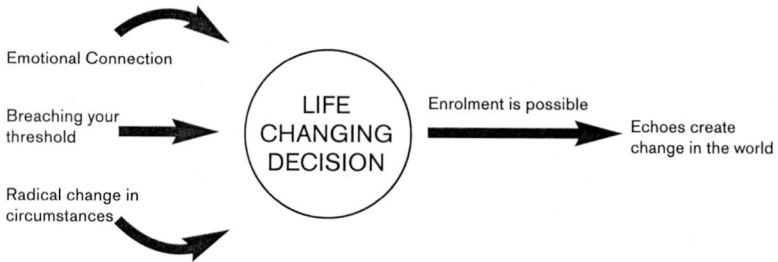

Emotional Connection

Breaching your threshold → LIFE CHANGING DECISION → Enrolment is possible → Echoes create change in the world

Radical change in circumstances

Not all three triggers need to occur simultaneously; sometimes just one of the three could result in a life-changing decision if the emotion associated with it is strong enough. Sometimes it may feel like all three triggers have fired – this is all right too. The circumstances around which those triggers might occur are different for everyone – from watching something on television, reading something, hearing something that you vehemently disagree with, or being physically or emotionally affected by something – it could move you into making a decision that you would not have considered under normal conditions. There are also people who wake up one day and just make a decision with no external prompts or drivers that they could attribute their realisation to. That's great for them, but for the rest of us who might need help accelerating to our tipping points, the techniques described below may be helpful to consider.

Taking each trigger in turn, here are the conditions I believe need to be in place for long-lasting decisions to be made, for enrolment to be effective and for echoes in the world to be created:

A deep emotional connection – 'I must do ...'

This occurs when you hear, touch, feel, or see something that creates a deep emotional connection to a positive outcome. It could have been something that was lingering and the experience of the incident 'tips' you over. For example, you may have been thinking about exercising for a long time, and then when someone close to you reports a positive outcome, it results in you taking action. It creates the 'I must do xyz' in you. The event might also be a negative, for example, you witnessed or watched on television cruelty to an animal, and it prompted you to volunteer your time at or make a donation to a local charity. This emotional connection is like shifting gears in a car – it prepares you for motion, it gets you to notice something, to sit up and pay attention. It triggers emotion, creating new neural pathways which moves you to act. A core value is being exercised or a key need of yours is being met when you take action, and it feels wonderful. In some circumstances you may not be able to rationalise or explain the feeling. You feel a strong sense of purpose, meaning and fulfilment. There is alignment – you, with your higher purpose. Although the event itself may have been far from pleasant, you have a good feeling about the outcome you want to achieve, and you work tirelessly toward achieving it. Your actions may be perceived by some as being ludicrous, and by others as admirable, but if you believe in it, then take action. People will see this, and the right people will be inspired to support you.

151

If this rings a bell for you, think about the following: what items, people, and circumstances do you need to source or gather, in order to create this emotional connection? What leverage do you need to make this decision stick? In the context of the new world, this may mean admitting that the recipe that you have been following for your life is not going to get you to where you want to be. It may mean dealing with much more emotional turmoil to get back on-track with the life you must lead. It makes you focus. This is where 'shoulds' are converted to 'must dos.' So I ask again: what must you do now to connect with your true purpose in life?

I mentioned earlier Tony Robbins' six basic human needs: certainty, variety, love, significance, personal development / growth, community. The pace at which your must-dos materialise into reality depends on the extent to which they relate to these six human needs. Now we can toddle along, living unfulfilled lives, waiting for an event at some point in the future to make an appearance and trigger the emotional connection, or we can create it ourselves right now. The choice is yours.

GUIDELINES FOR GETTING TO YOUR 'I MUST DO'

You will need a quiet spacious room; some dramatic music – classical or rock, something that has a powerful crescendo; cushions or pillows; and something to take notes with.

The process to follow involves thinking about the situation in your life that you are not happy about. Feel the emotion. Now intensify the emotion. Imagine another 10 years going by with the same situation occurring. Make it worse, bleaker, more strenuous. Notice the tension in your body – where does your body hold tension, and what does it feel like? Give it a name, and associate an image with it, if you can.

Now ask yourself the following questions:

- 😊 What is the pay-off for keeping this situation in your life?
- 😊 What have you sacrificed as a result of this?
- 😊 What would it be like if you continued living like this?
- 😊 Why change now?
- 😊 What exactly do you need to change?

Write down the answers to these questions. Take time to reflect. Say the answers out loud. Consider the impact and implications in your life.

Now think of the change as if it has already happened. Imagine what it would feel like if you have overcome the obstacles preventing you from living the life of your dreams? As you think it through, move around the room, increase your heart rate, which in turn will increase circulation. Breathe deeply. Speak, write and draw out your responses to the questions above while moving around – this activates the brain in coming up with new possibilities for you. Add anything new that comes up for you.

In some cases you may need to release anger or frustration – give the pillow a squeeze or a punch if you need to. Let out a scream if you need to – again use the pillow to mask the sound if you have to, to avoid the neighbours worrying! As you let go the negative emotion, focus on the positive feelings associated with your goal.

Now ask yourself the following questions:

- 😊 What are all the aspects of support you need to stick to the change?
- 😊 There is only one real thing you need to change? What is it?

☺ How committed are you to make that change?

☺ What support or leverage do you need to stick to that change?

At the point at which you hear the crescendo of the music (play it over if you need to), make that change immediately. Whatever you have written, act now. Even if all of it can't be done, do one thing that gets you closer to achieving the whole change. It might be a phone call, an e-mail, a photograph, do something, do one thing immediately.

Take a moment to fill yourself with a sense of accomplishment in taking an action that moves you a step closer to what you want to achieve. Now celebrate!

Breaching your threshold – 'I've had enough'

Sometimes we find ourselves in environments that are simply awful. Whether we are products of circumstance, whether we chose incorrectly, whether we were forced into this environment, it does not matter. Maybe you are being abused by a parent or loved one, maybe you are struggling to make ends meet, or maybe you are just feeling let down by the system. When you get to the point of feeling, 'I've had enough', you're at the point of zero tolerance. And this is a very good place to be. You realise you can no longer afford or can no longer bear to continue on this path. That volcanic eruption that needs releasing happens now. As you interrupt old habits, you open yourself up to creating new ones. It doesn't matter that you may not yet even know what to do next. You may or may not have an idea, but one thing's for sure, you've had enough of what you currently have, and you need to try something different, immediately.

It may seem reckless to people looking at you from the outside, as you deal with the frustration, but when you are at this point the emotion is so powerful that it also prompts the 'now'; it brings urgency to the action you need to take. An example of this would be a battered wife who is tipped over the edge by that last blow from an abusive husband. Or the doting father, who is denied access to his children because his estranged wife is using the children as pawns in a bid for money and control. The anger, frustration, despair drives the aggrieved to act immediately. When anger becomes the predominant feeling, heart rates, blood pressure and adrenaline climb. The body prepares for fight or flight responses. Learning how to channel this emotion into something positive is critical to achieving the best outcome. Finding the strength and the courage to walk away from toxic relationships: the battered wife focuses on rebuilding her self-esteem; the doting father focuses on how to maintain contact with his children. Their courage inspires the same in others. It shows that change can be achieved. They become polarised against what they no longer desire, and toward what they focus on next for their lives.

So, rather than wait for that painful last blow, here's how to get to 'I've had enough' and still move forward.

GUIDELINES FOR GETTING TO 'I'VE HAD ENOUGH'

Using the same scene set as above – space, music, writing material and technique – ask yourself these questions and record your answers:

- ☺ There is something in your life that is causing you suffering. What is it?
- ☺ Where in your body do you feel the suffering?
- ☺ What emotion are you feeling as a result of the suffering being in your life?
- ☺ On a scale of 1 to 10, where 10 is extremely intense, how would you rate your feelings?
- ☺ What would happen if the negatives in your life continued?

Now intensify the suffering. Describe it as an object. Give it weight, volume, texture. Now imagine that you have to keep this in your life for another 10 years.

- ☺ How do you feel?
- ☺ (Before you ask the next question, start moving around the room.) What do you want for your life? Quickly make your wish list.
- ☺ I want you to believe for a moment that you can have everything on your wish list. Now stop for a minute. Of all the thoughts you have had, items you have listed, and rankings you have provided on the scale above, I want you to find the one thing you need to make the decision to change your life around. What is it? (Replay the crescendo of the music at this point as many times as necessary). Repeat the exercise frequently until you come up with potential solutions.
- ☺ Visualise that you have achieved everything on your wish-list. How do you feel? (Now celebrate).
- ☺ When can you take your first step?

This exercise is designed to acknowledge the negative situation in your life, but get you focused on what you actually want to achieve. Moving away from something can have you move in circles, which is not ideal. Moving towards something is far more effective in achieving what you want for your future.

A radical change in circumstances – 'I have no choice'
The third trigger which enables a life changing decision to be made is where the floor of your world has seemingly fallen away, leaving you feeling like 'I have no choice'. It forces you to make a change,

even though it may be extremely difficult letting go of the past. Perhaps you were made redundant from your job, or your business went bankrupt. Maybe you sustained a debilitating injury or you encountered the death of a loved one or a parent, or perhaps a spouse who provided for you financially. Whatever the event, it has altered the course of your life suddenly. You are forced to do something radically different. In some cases you know what needs to be done; in others you genuinely don't. You need to take a step, but your legs won't let you. In fact your whole body may feel like jelly, you don't have the strength, or confidence or maybe even the ability. You can't find the will. It's an innate terror that grips you, and you are paralysed. You don't have the luxury of time to muster courage or gather your wits – taking action quickly is critical, maybe because someone is depending on you.

When your floor has fallen away, and you feel yourself falling, floundering, arms flailing, this is when you look up, muster all the faith left in you, and fly! It's a deliberate choice you make. Wave those arms wildly, and use the force of the wind to carry you. Eventually you will soar, but initially you have to just have faith and *do* something.

Some people, however, accept the default position. They fall. Some people are crippled by pain, and falling is inescapable; I empathise with that. If you choose to fall, I will respect that. Some people thrive on falling – the drama of it makes for a good story. However, if you must fall, I am going to ask you to prepare yourself to bounce back at a point in time – an hour, a day, a week – because hitting rock bottom and staying there is no longer an option. Time is merciless. It waits for no one. Ask for help if you are having trouble bouncing back. The very point at which you feel that you don't have what it takes, or when you are at your lowest point, is the point at which you do something. You do anything. You do everything. And you will rise, like the Phoenix rose from the ashes.

John Fisher's Personal Transition Curve, revised in 2012 and based on his work in constructivist theory, is a good illustration of the stages individuals go through when faced with personal change. It describes feelings of anxiety when things are not going so well; happiness when you believe a solution is in sight; feeling fearful, slightly threatened or in denial are natural next stages as you consider the ramifications of the change, and there are even occasions when you feel a sense of guilt for effecting certain situations. Feeling disillusioned and possibly even depressed are the ultimate lows – if somehow you get there, I would encourage you to bounce back, or seek help from a medical practitioner if you're there for an extended period. Gradually you move into an acceptance stage, believing in either yourself or something that will make the situation better. It is from this place of acceptance, that change can really be made. You have to decide from here what you want. Very often we focus on what we don't want and we don't really go far, and yet we are confused by the lack of progress. Once you have decided what you want to achieve, take action immediately. This is critical.

For the loss of a loved one, I absolutely accept and support that everyone needs to go through the grief cycle, and Elisabeth Kübler-Ross' model of grief is well placed to deal with this. Grief is human. It's absolutely necessary. No one has a right to tell someone else how long is appropriate for them to mourn a loss. That's unique to the individual concerned. I respect that entirely.

Similarly people who have been diagnosed with depression or other mental or anxiety disorders will have been prescribed a course of therapy and medication, and each process is specific to the individual concerned.

However, when it comes to other life changes such as debilitating injuries, loss of limbs, bankruptcy, needing to work again or take up a job after decades because you're left with no other choice, well, I know that can be scary. And I know that even if you've worked really hard to get to the acceptance stage, deciding what you want next can be hard and taking that first step towards what you want can be even harder.

Acceptance does not automatically mean the removal of fear and uncertainty, so here are two interventions that I believe need to be taken to neutralise the effects of feeling 'I have no choice'.

GUIDELINES FOR GETTING TO 'I HAVE INFINITE CHOICES'

- ☺ Separate the emotion from the issue and deal with the issue. Easier written than done, so you may need to work on the emotion first before dealing with the issue. By doing this, you will create a clearing in your mind and will be able to tap into your creative side – which we all have. Emotions are a good thing. They send you signals that inform your responses. They are designed to help you, and not control you. We sometimes find ourselves in situations where we are controlled by our emotions. This is not ideal and needs to be addressed.
- ☺ Deal with the emotions. Examine the 'motivation' of your emotion. How is it serving you? Where an emotion causes negativity or prolonged anxiety or frustration, it may be necessary to neutralise it. There are a variety of techniques that can help you to manage emotions more effectively.

Neuro-linguistic Programming – the 'Swish' Technique is a popular emotional control technique, which centres on replacing unwanted thoughts or responses with more positive ones, thereby achieving focus on what is required, rather than what is not required.

The Emotional Management Method, which I have personally trained in, developed by Patryk & Kasia Wezowski, is similar to the previous methods; it replaces an unwanted thought or response with a more appropriate one, making use of visual imagery and using each hand to 'grasp' desired, and 'release' unwanted emotions.

Emotional Freedom Tapping Technique has been around for quite a while, although there is little scientific evidence to support it. The emotional intensity is scored and monitored with each 'round' of tapping specific areas of the body around the eye and the collar bone.

The Sedona Method is a technique geared to help people release unwanted feelings and emotions using a series of questions, which enable people to place each situation in perspective and act on it appropriately.

Cognitive Behavioural Therapy (CBT) is a highly effective way of reprogramming current thinking patterns and beliefs in order to establish repeating behaviours which generate the desired results. What stands out for me about CBT is its sustainability over the long term.

Visualisation is used in many ways but almost always to achieve movement towards something desired. Some psychologists believe that if we are able to see it first and think it through, we will handle stressful situations more positively. Imagine yourself reacting calmly and confidently in a situation that normally causes you upset. Turn it over in your mind until it feels both believable and achievable. Your brain will believe it has experience in dealing with it, and will therefore help you respond appropriately.

The Freeze Frame® Technique is a minute-long technique developed by Doc Childre (founder of the Institute of HeartMath®) and Howard

Martin. It encourages a major shift in perception, centring more on a 'heart' rather than 'head' approach.

As a specialist of change, I know that the only way to move toward the change, to keep moving, and to not revert back to old ways, is to change your association toward the issue but to also be clear on what you want and why. By doing this, you will engage your mind in coming up with a solution and/or developing the courage to move forward. Robbins teaches that people fear making decisions to change as they associate pleasure with their old behaviours even though the consequences may be detrimental. For example, someone may wish to lose weight, but associate exercise with pain, and unhealthy food as pleasurable. For neuro-associative conditioning techniques to work, two beliefs need to drive behaviour: that you have the power and ability to make change happen in your life, and that change can occur immediately.

Robbins describes a 5-step process for neuro-associative conditioning to work. The first step is making that 'decision' – committing to the change in your life that you want to see. The second step he describes is obtaining leverage on your decision. Leverage entails finding positives to work towards and negatives to move away from. The third step entails interrupting habits or patterns of thinking, speech and behaviour by doing something spontaneous that shifts focus. For example, in his book, *Awaken the Giant Within*,' he says. '*Next time you start to feel depressed, jump up, look at the sky, and yell in your most idiotic tone of voice, "Hallelujah! My feet don't stink today!" A stupid, silly move like that will definitely shift your attention.*'

Robbins compares interrupting patterns to scratching a record so that it will no longer play properly. Having done this, it is important to create a new pattern – the fourth step. This prevents reverting back to old habits and creates the opportunity for a new way of being. Repeating the new pattern will reinforce it, until it becomes a constructive habit is important. Finally, Robbins challenges us to test the new behaviour, by placing ourselves in the situation where the destructive behaviour is likely to occur. Ensuring that the new pattern is applied, instead of the old one, ensures that you are on the right track.

Applying Robbins' neuro-associative-conditioning, here are my tips on how to shift the paradigm of 'I have no choice' to 'I have infinite choices'. Consider the situation you were in when all was fine, and you were happy. Now list all the limitations of that situation – the compromises you made, the sacrifices, the lost time, the missed opportunities.

Now consider the situation you are in now. List all the fears, anxieties or frustrations you have with the situation you are now faced with. Work through them using the techniques described above (CBT, NLP Swish). List all the positive opportunities this situation presents you with. This may be tough to do in the beginning. Give it the time that is needed, but stick with it. Don't give up. Describe how these opportunities might be aligned to achieving purpose in your life. Describe how these opportunities might help you realise your true potential. Describe how these opportunities might help you discover innate talents.

Amidst the trepidation, feel excited by it; just a little at a time will do. Think about how amazing it will be if you could actually achieve your hearts desires. What is that one step you need to take toward making a change? Is that the first step? What is the first step? Now just take a deep breath, and take that first step. Feel the excitement of transforming your life into something better than it has ever been. Breathe, feel the step, stabilise yourself. What's the next step? Again take a physical step. Enjoy the feeling. The butterflies or anxiety you may be feeling is perfectly normal. Stick with it. Just focus on the excitement that may be buried somewhere within you. It's there – find it.

Now it may be that you don't know what you want. This is perfectly okay, use the process to simply get you closer to discovering what it is that you need to do. For example, take the step to contact someone or undertake some research which might help you unleash what's been hidden in you all along.

Look at this from a different perspective. Do you really believe you are on this planet and have no choices? Completing this exercise, and repeating it if you have to, will neutralise feelings of hopelessness and helplessness. You will get to a place of realising that you must take action.

Hopefully you will have recognised yourself in these situations, and are well on your way to making that life-changing decision.

Enrolment, the consequence of making a life-changing decision, is critical for the future: we can't build the world alone. We can't come up with solutions alone. You cannot enrol people unless they have made conscious decisions about their lives which align with what you are standing for. This is how you will achieve sustainable change and growth. In order for people to make life-changing decisions, they need to experience a deep emotional connection to what you are saying, doing and standing for. They need to have gotten to the end of their tether with something in their lives; and/or they need to have experienced a sudden and radical change in their lives that left them with no choice but to change. Deciding on what next is often a challenge in itself, keeping people stuck in an unhealthy situation for longer than necessary. If their decision aligns with your intentions, then enrolment is possible. Enrolment spawns creativity and valour which in turn creates echoes. Echoes inspire and encourage more of the same and better to be done. It tones down the negative talk and amplifies greater positivity.

Enrolment is about making that life-changing decision which attracts like-minded people to your vision. The energy and excitement creates echoes, which in turn become contagious. Imagine a world where we are all enthusiastically engaged in something that requires and delivers positive outcomes. A fool's errand, sceptics may say. Remember,

'All truth passes through three stages.
First, it is ridiculed.
Second, it is violently opposed.
Third, it is accepted as being self-evident.'
ARTHUR SCHOPENHAUER, GERMAN PHILOSOPHER (1788 – 1860)

Moral of the story – stick with what you believe in; eventually people will come around, and enrolment of the right people will occur.

TEN

CONCLUSION

Some people love the hum-drum of Mumbai and, being Indian, I should have too, but I didn't – although I am determined to go back soon to change that perception. A colleague and I were there on business for a week. On our very last day we had a few hours to spare before we caught our flight back to London, so we walked through one of the touristy streets whose pavements were lined with little stalls of people selling goods for their livelihood. We were following the masses of shoppers, browsing the stalls, and only half paying attention to what was going on around us as we tried to block out the honking horns, the smells and the pleas of the desperate sellers. As the crowds of people in front of me stepped over something, I did the same, except as I did, it moved.

Startled, I looked down and to my horror saw a 4-month old baby girl on the pavement. She was on her side, desperately reaching for her dry, dirty bottle which had clearly been kicked out of her little hands by one of the passers-by.

Her face was dry, her lips chapped, and all she wore was a tiny vest which did little to protect her skin from the harsh heat and jagged surface of the well-worn pavement she lay on, her skin scratched and knees torn. She didn't even have on a diaper. I stopped in horror, and my first instinct was to reach down and pick up the child. My colleague held me back. I fought her off. She tugged me away. I couldn't make sense of what I was more angered about – the practically naked little girl left unattended on the street or my colleague not allowing me, or her not wanting to help this helpless baby. I tore away from her, and rushed back to where the little girl was – only this time noticing a 5-year old boy trying to pick her up, although now she was crying, perhaps from not having her dry bottle, or possibly even someone having stepped on her or tripped over her. I tore off the jumper I wore around my shoulders, and put it around the little girl. I asked the little boy where her mother was. He replied in Hindi and I couldn't understand. I looked around for someone to translate. There were so many people around, but no one seemed concerned, and no one responded to my pleas for help. The little boy wanted to tell me something. The little baby girl reached out to me. He wouldn't let me take her, even though he struggled to hold her. I rushed to the closest street seller to ask him to translate for me. He offered me two handbags to buy then swore me off, in English and Hindi, when I ignored the handbags. I went to the next and the next and no one would translate. The little boy watched me with sad eyes I remember, the little girl desperately reaching out to me, tears washing the dust off her face. She rubbed her eyes and I could see it hurt as more sand got into her eyes. I wondered whether she thought I was her mother. After what seemed like hours of frantically trying to get the attention of passers-by and market sellers, a shopkeeper came outside, held me firmly by the arm, ushering me to the side, and told me definitively to stop making a scene. Then he translated for me.

The little girl was being watched by her 5-year old uncle. The boy's sister, the mother of the little girl, who was only 14 years old, worked nearby. Work meant prostitution (unbeknown to the little boy), the shopkeeper told me matter of factly. It was likely that if I touched or carried the child, then 'the watchers' would demand money aggressively from me. He showed me all the children in the nearby vicinity in a similar predicament. My mind could not comprehend. Having been brought up in Chatsworth, I thought I'd seen poverty. Never like this.

I asked what he or anyone else did to help the children as they sat on the sidewalk all day. He shrugged his shoulders. He claimed there was nothing he could do, because if he did, more children would appear needing help and that would not be sustainable. He already had a family of his own, and had to take in the family of his wife's sister too. He gave me the details of a nearby police station, but before I left, I bought some soap, diapers, antiseptic and band-aids and I showed the little boy how to clean the little girl's torn skin. The shopkeeper let me wash and clean the little girl's bottle, filling it with milk that I purchased from him. She sucked on it thirstily, staring into the little boy's face.

A nearby stall was selling baby clothes, so I bought her something to wear and a blanket that would shield her from the harsh pavement. As the stall owner took my money, he said in broken English, 'You are wasting your time. Tomorrow she will have no clothes again – how else will her mother get people like you to pay?' I was horrified. That the family could be that desperate; that the child would not benefit from the clothes for longer than a day; that the stall owner believed I was wasting my time.

I bought food for the little boy which he carefully broke into six pieces. I watched curiously. He then flung his head back and screeched out loud, his little voice extremely powerful for this thin frame. In no time five other little boys and girls of a similar age came running toward him. They grabbed the food and ran off just as quickly as they arrived. He was left with barely a bite but he savoured every last crumb. I bought more food, kept just enough money to pay for the taxi-fare back to the hotel and airport and gave the rest to the little boy and some to the shopkeeper, asking him if he would feed the children for the next few days, although I prayed they would not be there for that long, that somehow Child Services will have collected them by then. His eyes lit up as he took the money and he said that he would. I needed to believe that he would. Later, when talking to the desk sergeant at the police station, I was left with less confidence that anything would be done. Crushing.

I vaguely remember the point at which I resigned myself to heading back to the hotel. As I stepped into the taxi I seemed to have stepped into a time-warp as well. That hamster wheel called my life had been increasing in size and speed for many years, I kept going faster and faster but in this moment I realised it held no meaning. What exactly was I working for, if little children were on the street like this?

I had made an emotional connection with all those people: the masses of crowds who ignored the value of human life, the stall owner, the watchers, the shopkeeper, the children, and most importantly the little girl who changed my life. The value of human life seemed to have gotten lost somewhere along those noisy streets of Mumbai.

I realised that day that I had lost something too. Somewhere in the race of life that I got entangled in, I had lost sight of my vision for my life. I had lost my connection to my purpose in life, and that's when the emptiness crept in.

I flew into Heathrow, numb from my experience in Mumbai. I went straight to my client for another relatively insignificant day's work, lugging my suitcase up stairs, and downstairs, carrying, lifting. It was heavy, it was full. Yet I felt so empty. That suitcase carried my conscience from Mumbai to Tottenham Court Road Station. I didn't realise how lost I was until I found myself on the kitchen floor the next morning – the day my back broke. I realised during my long recovery that I *must* take care of myself no matter what; that *I had had enough* of pretending that life was all right as it was, but most importantly I realised that *I had no choice but* to play a role in making a change to the lives of children, people, animals and the planet, using my brain, my mind, my hands, my feet and every cell in my body. It was then that I had decided to move back to South Africa, and the rest is *not* as they say history, but a present for my future!

You now know the full story of my life: my humble beginnings, my lessons, life's blessings; my travels, the suitcase, my baggage; losing my way, finding my way, Tottenham Court Road Station; the value of my back injury, and ultimately the little girl in Mumbai who changed my life by bringing me full circle. She reminded me of what truly matters in this world. She reminded me of the vision I had set for myself: to be free. In order for me to be free I had to ultimately help people find their freedom ... so that no more little boys and girls are left hungry and unattended on any streets anywhere in the world in future.

That is my story.
This is my life.

With 2 billion more people likely to inhabit this planet by 2040, we are fooling ourselves into thinking that somehow the world's problems will solve themselves. By 2040 we simply cannot have children on the streets, suffering from malnutrition, women prostituting themselves, people dying prematurely of diseases like HIV and other sexually transmitted diseases. We cannot continue to educate as we do. We need more robust solutions for food, water and energy provisioning. We need to preserve the environment as well, protecting animals and wildlife. We need to engage the hearts and minds of the people in this world to make a change.

I want to see a world where everyone on the planet has envisioned a life that includes the wellbeing of others and the planet. I want us to engage the power of our enquiring minds to come up with real solutions for a struggling human race. We need more entrepreneurial minds like the Bransons, Gates and Winfreys to run countries instead of companies, and bash the bureaucracy out of governments.

I want us to interact with each other with high degrees of emotional intelligence: love, acceptance and compassion, inspiring greatness in each other, rather than assassinating characters and crucifying creativity. I want to kick out smug educators and kick start what real expertise should deliver. I want extraordinarily ordinary people like you and me to make deliberate choices about the environment, preserving the planet's resources and changing our habits to more sustainable practices. I want to see us protect animals with every breath left in us.

If we are to fail, let it be at something incredible, rather than the profound failure of common sense.

I want to live and work among selfless people who express gratitude daily for the high and low tides of life, and who bring peak focus to exercising their minds and their bodies for the betterment of what lies beyond selfish gain. I want to smash through the walls that keep people's imaginations and innovations imprisoned. I want us to actively choose life and leave behind the wastelands of procrastination and greed. I want to surgically remove the tumours of doubt that keep us content with the suffering that engulfs us. I want to douse the flames of envy and ignite the fires of passion in a common belief that we can make a difference. I want to collaborate with like-minded people, each of us enrolling the other into the possibility of creating a new world that delivers an exponential improvement in the quality of life without any one of the planet's inhabitants being disadvantaged.

I want this message to echo around the world. Help me do this. Start with yourself, since only you can. Allow yourself to tap into your infinite mind today.

'Be the change in the world you want to see,'

MAHATMA GANDHI (1869 – 1948)

Your future starts now.

Welcome to The Mind Age™.

ACKNOWLEDGEMENTS

This book is inspired by the balance of life: good and bad, joy and sorrow, fear and love. Too many people were complaining, too many people ill, too many people giving up, and too many people settling for less than they were worth.

I wanted to do something to help the situation: sharing some of my life experiences and including perspectives of world and industry experts will, I hope, help. This book would not have been possible without the incredible people in my life.

To Lucy McCarraher, my editor and publisher. Thank you for your genius, your patience, and your straight-talk. Words just don't seem adequate to express my gratitude to you for your patience and flexibility in making this happen for me. I could not have done this without you.

To Gerard O'Donovan, one of my greatest mentors. This phase of my life started because of you. You made it sound easy: building a successful and sustainable coaching business, running a magazine, writing a book, international virtual teams, high energy, major impact. All of this achieved within one year. You were right. It can be done. I cannot thank you enough. You are simply amazing, and I am so fortunate to have you in my life.

To my nieces, Raeesa and Nadine: Concordia will never have sailed or flown as famously as it has for as long as it has, had it not been for you. To think that one of our 'London Lunches' was all that it took to breathe life into Concordia is mind-boggling. Why am I then surprised that *The Mind Age*™ was conceived at the next 'London Lunch', and every chapter that followed developed from every 'London Lunch' after that! You are truly incredible women – and destined for many great things. Thank you for all the ideas, challenge and support, but most importantly for all the fun we have when we are together. Long may that continue!

Doctor Nadine Hoosen, that you would text me randomly with ideas or suggestions amidst hectic schedules at the hospital; that you would find the time to listen to me, work with me to formulate ideas and later test the models and frameworks that we came up with; that you found the energy to proof-read the manuscript and its iterations on numerous occasions, and still do this in a constructive way, after 36-hour shifts. You leave me in awe! I hope you feel the book represents our collective brainpower. I am very blessed to have you in my life.

My niece Tizaya, thank you for keeping me on-track: for encouraging me during those times when I was ready to shelve the manuscript for another year, for contributing ideas, and for kicking my butt at just the right times. I couldn't have gotten it over the finish line without you.

My niece Nadia, you helped me keep the book real. You brought an edge to it, and I appreciate that very much. Thank you for the realism you brought and for the constructive criticism.

Claire, Nicola, Ethan, Lea and Teeyana – looking through your eyes I learnt so much. I hope that you relate to this book in a way that inspires you to keep the revolution going in your generation to change the world for the better, one person at a time.

Lyn, Debbie and Trevor, thank you for your unique perspectives in helping me deliver a quality story. Thank you for believing in me and for encouraging me to see it through. I know it looked like I was bumming around for a while, but I assure you, it was part of my creative process! (I'm sure by now you realise, as the youngest, and by a significant margin I might add, I can still get away with everything, or can at least outrun you if I can't!) I love you lots.

To Alison Abu, Sean Sankey and David Warne, who taught me about unconditional love, acceptance and forgiveness. Thank you that I can be completely myself when I am with you. Even during the times when I go off the radar for months at a time, you respect my 'process' and still love me when I resurface. You are so special to me.

To the rest of my dear friends – thank you for allowing me into your lives. Thank you for helping me shape and build Concordia into something that facilitates breakthroughs in people's lives. Thank you for being there for me, for encouraging and supporting. You are truly amazing. My life could never be what it is now without you being a part of it. I sincerely hope we stay friends for life.

To all my extended family – I hope you know that you are my treasure! No words can describe how much you mean to me. It shouldn't matter whether we've seen each other recently or spoken – just know that you have been a huge part of my life and shaped who I am today. I am so grateful to have had your love, care and support. May you be blessed always.

Andrew Crossey, Senior Vice President and Global Talent Management Director for Capgemini Consulting, my mentor and an exemplar of only the best leadership qualities on the planet. Andy, thank you for the unique perspectives you provided for this book. I have no doubt this wave has already been set in motion, and with people like you driving it, the world can only become a better place. On a personal level, thank you for always taking the 'let's put the kettle on' approach to solving the dramas that life dealt us when we worked together. At a critical time in my life you stood by me and believed in me when I didn't or couldn't find the will to. I will never forget that. You are my real life super-hero.

Marc Kahn and Dr. Adam Gordon: I realise how odd it must have been receiving a random e-mail from someone you didn't know asking for you to contribute to a book I could tell you nothing about. Thank you for trusting me to bring your opinions to life. I sincerely hope that we can take this forward together in South Africa and eventually all of Africa – in industry, in education, in life.

Douglas Umbers and Alan Richell: thank you for providing me with your perspectives for this book. I appreciate your faith in me. I look forward to working more closely with you in future in making these ideas a reality.

To the most influential teachers throughout my school life and beyond: Mrs. P. Naidoo, Mrs. M. Govender, Mrs Bramdeow, Mrs. S. Lachman, Ms. N.D. Naidoo, Mrs. Ramduki, Mrs. T. Naidoo, Mr. Archary, from Tyburn Primary, Sunnyvale Primary, and Centenary Secondary. Moira Redman, what an incredible role model you were. I will never forget you. Tony Maurice, you are one in a billion! Thank you for all the support despite the distance and time. I am working on my filters! To all the phenomenal women in my life – you have been an incredible force in shaping who I am today. Please know that you are admired and appreciated.

To all the many interviewees, especially Shakeer's family, who contributed various perspectives to the book – thank you for believing in the cause, for wanting to make a difference, for making a contribution. I hope that your stories echo across the generations and inspire greatness.

To my dogs, Jazzy, Lucy and Riley, for having been so understanding and patient with me whilst I wrote this book. You make me laugh every day and you show me the true meaning of unconditional love. Thank you for teaching me how to shake things off. I owe you loads of cuddles, and now that the book is done, loads of walkies!

To Shakeer, you are such a mix of wisdom and silliness. I question our future every day but there's no denying what an incredible life we've had so far. Thank you for supporting my dream, for encouraging me every step of the way, and for giving me the space and the time to uncover the best version of myself. I am very fortunate to have you in my life.

To my mum, thank you for dedicating your life to ensuring that we are the best we could be. You instilled in us a deep sense of belief in ourselves, along with strong morals and values. You always put us first, and always gave us your best in order to bring out our best. Thank you for always caring, for always maintaining the 'mum' standards and for helping us never lose sight of the goal.

And finally to my dad, the scientist, the artist, the mathematician, and the best dad anyone could ask for. Thank you for always having been there to see me through my most challenging life experiences. Thank you for helping me get Concordia up, running and soaring to great heights. Thank you also for supporting me with this book. I could not have asked for anything more from you, and yet you continue to give all that you have and more. Thank you for the tough-love always. It made all the difference. Had I not had your influence in my life I would not have been curious to explore my mind.

REFERENCES

Byrne, Rhonda, 2006. The Secret. Hardcover edition. New York: Atria Books/Beyond Words; 1st Atria Books/Beyond Words

Canterucci, Jim, 2005. Personal Brilliance: Mastering the Everyday Habits That Create a Lifetime of Success. Hardcover edition. New York: AMACOM

Carson, Rachel, 1962. Silent Spring. Hardcover edition 2002. New York: Houghton Mifflin Harcourt

Covey, Stephen R., 2000. The 7 Habits of Highly Effective People (Miniature Edition). Running Press Miniature Editions; Min edition

Dale, Edgar. Audio-Visual Methods in Teaching, 3rd ed., Holt, Rinehart & Winston, New York, 1969, p. 108

Del Gatto, Susan J., 2009. Creating Balance in a World of STRESS: Six Key Habits to Avoid in order to Reduce Stress. Paperback edition 2009. iUniverse

Dossey, Larry, 2009. The Power of Premonitions: How Knowing the Future Can Shape Our Lives. Kindle Edition 2009. USA: Penguin Group

Drucker, Peter, 2012. Innovation & Entrepreneurship. Kindle Edition. Routledge.

Eker, T. Harv, 2005. Secrets of the Millionaire Mind: Mastering the Inner Game of Wealth. Hardcover 1st edition. New York: HarperBusiness

Frankl, Viktor E., Winslade, William J., Kushner, Harold S., 1959.

Man's Search for Meaning. Mass Market Paperback 2006. USA:
Beacon Press

Gardner, Howard, 1983. Frames of Mind: The Theory of Multiple
Intelligences. Paperback edition 2011. New York: Basic Books

Gladwell, Malcolm, 2002. The Tipping Point: How Little Things
Can Make a Big Difference. Paperback edition. Abacus

Gladwell, Malcolm, 2008. Outliers: The Story of Success. Reprent
edition 2011. Back Bay Books

Goleman, Daniel, 1998. Working with Emotional Intelligence.
Paperback edition 2000. USA: Bantam Book

Goleman, Daniel, 2011. Leadership: The Power of Emotional
Intelligence. Kindle 1st digital edition 2011. Michigan:More Than
Sound LLC

Goleman, Daniel, 2011. The Brain and Emotional Intelligence: New
Insights. Kindle 1st edition 2011. Michigan:More Than Sound LLC

Gordon, Adam, 2008. Future Savvy: identifying trends to make
better decisions, manage uncertainty, and profit from change.
Hardcover Edition 2008. New York: Amacom

Gore, Al, 2006. An Inconvenient Truth. Paperback First edition
2006. New York: Rodale Books

Gore, Al. 2009. Our Choice: A Plan to Solve the Climate Crisis. New
York: Penguin Group

Isaacson, Walter, 2011. Steve Jobs. Hardcover edition. New York:
Simon & Schuster

Kahn, Marc S. 2014. Coaching on the Axis. Paperback edition 2014.
London: Karnac Books

Kiyosaki, Robert T., 2001. Rich Dad Poor Dad: What The Rich

Teach Their Kids About Money That the Poor and Middle Class Do Not! Mass Market Paperback edition 2011. Plata Publishing

Kübler-Ross, Elisabeth, 2008. On Death 7 Dying: What the dying have to teach doctors, nurses, clergy and their own families. Revised Edition, Routledge.

NrBooks, 2013. Richard Branson Failure and Success: The history of a Billionaire. Paperback edition. CreateSpace Independent Publishing Platform

O'Neill, Gerard, 1989. The High Frontier. Paperback edition 1989. Los Angeles: Space Studies Institute

Payne, Wayne, 1985. Doctoral Paper on Emotions and Emotional Intelligence. The Union for Experimenting colleges and universities; 0557

Priestley, Daniel, 2013. Entrepreneur Revolution: How to develop your entrepreneurial mindset and start a business that works. Paperback 1st edition. United Kingdom: Capstone

Randers, Jorgen, 2012. 2052: A Global Forecast for the next forty years. Kindle Edition. Chelsea Green Publishing.

Ratey, John, 2008. Spark: The Revolutionary New Science of Exercise and the Brain. Reprint edition. Little Brown and Company

Reynolds, Gretchen, 2012. The First 20 Minutes: Surprising Science Reveals How We Can Exercise Better, Train Smarter, Live Longer. Paperback edition 2013. USA: Plume

Robbins, Tony, 1992. Awaken the Giant Within: How to Take Immediate Control of Your Mental, Emotional, Physical and Financial Destiny. 2003 Paperback edition New York: Free Press

Robbins, Tony, 1994. Giant Steps: Author Of Awaken The Giant And Unlimited Power. New York: Simon & Schuster

Salovey, Peter; Mayer, John; Caruso, David (2004), "Emotional Intelligence: Theory, Findings, and Implications", Psychological Inquiry: 197–215. Cambridge, United Kingdom. Cambridge University Press

Tolle, Eckhart, 1999. The Power of Now: A Guide to Spiritual Enlightenment. Paperback edition 2004. California: New World Library

Vanzant, Iyanla, 1998. One Day My Soul Just Opened Up: 40 Days and 40 Nights Toward Spiritual Strength and Personal Growth. Paperback edition. USA: Simon & Schuster

Williamson, Marianne, 1992. A Return to Love: Reflections on the Principles of "A Course in Miracles". Paperback edition 1996. USA: HarperOne

ONLINE REFERENCES

'The Consequences of Global Warming On Glaciers and Sea'
http://www.nrdc.org/globalwarming/fcons/fcons4.asp>

'Ice-free Arctic' Peter Wadhams
http://www.theguardian.com/environment/earth-insight/2013/jul/24/arctic-ice-free-methane-economy-catastrophe

'Melting permafrost called ticking time-bomb'
http://www.thestar.com/news/canada/2011/12/01/melting_permafrost_called_ticking_time_bomb.html

John Vidal 'Food shortages could force world into vegetarianism, warn scientists' August 26, 2014 [Online] Available, the Guardian
http://www.theguardian.com/global-development/2012/aug/26/food-shortages-world-vegetarianism

Research Gate
http://www.researchgate.net/post/It_is_estimated_that_in_2040_the_world_population_will_be_9_038_687_000_Will_the_world_economy_be_able_to_support_this_population

'2013 World Hunger and Poverty Facts and Statistics' July 27, 2013 [Online] Available
http://www.worldhunger.org/articles/Learn/world%20hunger%20facts%202002.htm

Hearty, Paul: 'Rising Seas Threaten Low-Lying Coastlines | Ecology Global Network' March 1, 2012
http://www.ecology.com/2012/03/01/rising-seas-threaten-low-lying-coastlines/

'The majority of new vehicles are plug-in electric, or hybrids'
http://www.futuretimeline.net/21stcentury/2030.htm#electric-cars-2030

'Emerging job titles of today'
http://www.futuretimeline.net/21stcentury/2030.htm#career

'The majority of new vehicles are plug-in electric, or hybrids'
http://www.futuretimeline.net/21stcentury/2030.htm#electric-cars-2030

'Workopolis research: Ten jobs that will not exist ten years from now –
Workopolis
http://www.workopolis.com/content/advice/article/workopolis-2013-research-ten-jobs-that-will-not-exist-ten-years-from-now/

Hammond, Ray: 'The World in 2030' (2007)

Chang, Anthony: 'The World in 2040: A Brief Glimpse' October 1,
2013 [Online] Available
http://peds2040.chocchildrens.org/world-2040-brief-glimpse/

'About News of Future'
http://www.newsoffuture.com/about_news_of_future.html

'Playlist (11 talks) What does the future look like?'
http://www.ted.com/playlists/85/what_does_the_future_look_like?ww
w.21school.ox.ac.uk

'Globalization' January 8, 2014 [Online] Available
http://en.wikipedia.org/wiki/Globalization

'World population' April 08, 2014 [Online] Available
http://en.wikipedia.org/wiki/World_population

'Projections of population growth' July 22, 2014 [Online] Available
http://en.wikipedia.org/wiki/Projections_of_population_growth

'25 Visionaries Who Created Empires From Virtually Nothing' July 24, 2008 http://www.businesspundit.com/25-visionaries-who-created-empires-from-virtually-nothing/2/

'25 Visionaries Who Created Empires From Virtually Nothing' July 24, 2008 http://www.businesspundit.com/25-visionaries-who-created-empires-from-virtually-nothing/3/

'Tomgram: Michael T. Klare, 2040 or Bust' September 10, 2013 http://www.tomdispatch.com/blog/175745/

'Oil shale' July 24, 2014 http://en.wikipedia.org/wiki/Oil_shale

Butler, Nick: 'The world in 2040' http://blogs.ft.com/nick-butler/2013/07/30/the-world-in-2040/

Pfeifer, Sylvia: 'Nuclear reactors: from waste to fuel' February 14, 2013 http://www.ft.com/intl/cms/s/0/3bc927b4-769c-11e2-ac91-00144feabdc0.html#axzz2qwOylnX4

'Ideas to Change the World' http://terrapower.com/pages/benefits

Moss, Laura: 'The 13 largest oil spills in history' July 16, 2010 http://www.mnn.com/earth-matters/wilderness-resources/stories/the-13-largest-oil-spills-in-history

Chazan, Guy: 'Demand for innovation in energy keeps growing' January 17, 2014 http://www.ft.com/cms/s/0/492c26fe-793e-11e3-b381-00144feabdc0.html#axzz2qwOylnX4

Pozen, Robert and Hamacher, Theresa: 'China must reform for life after the iron rice bowl' January 5, 2014 http://www.ft.com/cms/s/0/e6cc7574-667b-11e3-8675-00144feabdc0.html#axzz2qwOylnX4

Wild, Jane: 'Inquiry finds flaws in Heathrow's expansion plan' September 29, 2013 http://www.ft.com/intl/cms/s/0/1f8728d6-291a-11e3-8d19-00144feab7de.html#axzz2qwOylnX4

Forget banking, become a farmer. Elaine Moore
http://www.ft.com/intl/cms/s/0/b5e0ab48-e7db-11e2-9aad-00144feabdc0.html#axzz2qwOylnX4

Eker, T Harv: 'What Is Your Money Blueprint?'
http://www.selfgrowth.com/articles/what_is_your_money_blueprint.html

Nedeva, Maria: 'How to change your money blueprint?' July 011
http://www.themoneyprinciple.co.uk/HOW-TO-CHANGE-YOUR-MONEY-BLUEPRINT/

Kanner, Jamie: 'The $$$ Blueprint: 7 Ways to Change Your Money
Mindset Now' October 29, 2013 http://girlillawarfare.com/the-blueprint-7-ways-to-change-your-money-mindset-now/

Heathfield, Susan M.: 'Create Your Personal Vision Statement'
http://humanresources.about.com/od/success/a/personal_vision.htm

Gillespie-Brown, Jon: 'Why Write a Personal Vision Statement?'
February 21, 2012 http://www.tobeanentrepreneur.com/blog/building-a-personal-vision-statement/

'What is Enquiring Minds?'
http://www.enquiringminds.org.uk/what_is_enquiring_minds/

Blekos, Angela: 'Inquiry learning in the classroom'
https://www.youtube.com/watch?v=yj4CWu5DI0U

Latumahina, Donald: '4 Reasons Why Curiosity is Important and How
to Develop It' http://www.lifehack.org/articles/productivity/4-reasons-why-curiosity-is-important-and-how-to-develop-it.html

Wallen, Daniel: '10 Signs You're A Critical Thinker'
<http://www.lifehack.org/articles/productivity/10-signs-youre-critical-thinker.html

Canterucci, Jim: 'Curiosity'
http://www.mypersonalbrilliance.com/curiosity/

Kashdan, Todd: 'The Power of Curiosity' May 2010
http://experiencelife.com/article/the-power-of-curiosity/

Moon, Garrett: 'Why Curiosity is the Most Important Tool in
Business' http://todaymade.com/blog/the-most-important-tool-in-
business/

Perry, Bruce Duncan, M.D., Ph.D.: 'Curiosity: The Fuel of
Development'
http://teacher.scholastic.com/professional/bruceperry/curiosity.htm

Chernoff, Marc: '30 Things to Start Doing for Yourself'
http://www.marcandangel.com/2011/12/18/30-things-to-start-doing-
for-yourself/

Musallam, Ramsey: 'TED TALK: 3 rules to spark learning'
http://www.cyclesoflearning.com/

'What is Enquiring Minds?'
http://www.enquiringminds.org.uk/what_is_enquiring_minds/

Blekos, Angela: 'Inquiry learning in the classroom' April 23, 2013
https://www.youtube.com/watch?v=yj4CWu5DI0U

Latumahina, Donald: '4 Reasons Why Curiosity is Important and How
to Develop It' http://www.lifehack.org/articles/productivity/4-reasons-
why-curiosity-is-important-and-how-to-develop-it.html

Wallen, Daniel: '10 Signs You're A Critical Thinker'
http://www.lifehack.org/articles/productivity/10-signs-youre-critical-
thinker.html

Canterucci, Jim: 'Curiosity'
http://www.mypersonalbrilliance.com/curiosity/

Kashdan, Todd: 'The Power of Curiosity' May 2010
http://experiencelife.com/article/the-power-of-curiosity/

Moon, Garrett: 'Why Curiosity is the Most Important Tool in
Business' http://todaymade.com/blog/the-most-important-tool-in-
business/

Perry, Bruce Duncan, M.D., Ph.D.: 'Curiosity: The Fuel of
Development'
http://teacher.scholastic.com/professional/bruceperry/curiosity.htm

Chernoff, Marc: '30 Things to Start Doing for Yourself'
http://www.marcandangel.com/2011/12/18/30-things-to-start-doing-
for-yourself/

Musallam, Ramsey: 'TED TALK: 3 rules to spark learning'
http://www.cyclesoflearning.com/

Paul, Annie Murphy: 'How to Stimulate Curiosity' April 15, 2013
http://ideas.time.com/2013/04/15/how-to-stimulate-curiosity/

Adams, Angel and Papciak, Patricia: 'Curiosity as the Key to Lifelong
Learning' http://www.drangeladams.com/2011/05/curiosity-as-the-
key-to-lifelong-learning/

Willingham, Theresa: 'Celebrating and Inspiring Curiosity as a Key
Component in Learning'
http://www.ted.com/conversations/145/celebrating_and_inspiring_cu
ri.html

'Early childhood learning – 5 Ways to Develop Your Child's
Curiosity!' http://www.etllearning.com/for-parents/articles/5-ways-
develop-your-childs-curiosity

'Self-Mastery'
http://www.mindtools.com/pages/article/newCDV_23.htm

Le, Vanna: 'The World's 12 Most Powerful Entrepreneurs Of 2013' October 30, 2013
http://www.forbes.com/sites/vannale/2013/10/30/the-worlds-12-most-powerful-entrepreneurs/

'Famous Entrepreneurs'
http://www.biographyonline.net/business/top-10-entrepreneurs.html

Preston, Jack: 'The world's top 10 business leaders'
http://www.virgin.com/entrepreneur/worlds-top-10-business-leaders

Key, Stephen: '5 Qualities of Successful Entrepreneurs' August 12, 2013 http://www.entrepreneur.com/article/227776

'The Behavioral Traits Of A Successful Entrepreneur' June 4, 2012
http://www.forbes.com/sites/groupthink/2012/06/04/the-behavioral-traits-of-a-successful-entrepreneur/

'Entrepreneurial behaviour'
http://libweb.surrey.ac.uk/library/skills/Entrepreneurship/B722B322_1_section2.html

'IED Fellows Programme'
http://www.easybib.com/cite/pdf?url=https://workspace.imperial.ac.uk/innovationstudies/Public/IED%20Fellows%20Lecture%201.pdf

'Personality' http://en.wikipedia.org/wiki/Personality

Dougherty, Edmond John: '20 Skills That All Successful Entrepreneurs Have' January 22, 2014 http://www.businessinsider.com/skills-of-successful-entrepreneurs-2014-1

Martins, Ajaero Tony: 'How to Develop your Entrepreneurial skills'
http://www.mytopbusinessideas.com/develop-entrepreneurial-skills/

Belonwu, Valentine: 'How to Develop Your Entrepreneurial Skills – 20 Tips' May 21, 2013
http://businessgross.com/2013/05/21/entrepreneurial-skills/

Branson, Richard: 'Richard Branson: Five Secrets to Business Success' September 9, 2010 http://www.entrepreneur.com/article/217284

'Richard Branson: The Good, The Bad, and The Money Quotes – Part 3' http://www.businesspundit.com/?s=richard+branson

Brady, Tara: 'Business is booming! Sisters aged seven and four become Britain's youngest entrepreneurs selling sweets at pocket money prices' http://www.dailymail.co.uk/news/article-2538126/Sisters-seven-four-Britains-youngest-entrepreneurs-selling-sweets-pocket-money-prices.html#ixzz30k1F7KKZ

Grove, Jack: 'UK has 'lowest drop-out rate in Europe' April 1, 2014 http://www.timeshighereducation.co.uk/news/uk-has-lowest-drop-out-rate-in-europe/2012400.article

Sellgren, Katherine: 'Warning of worsening in UK skills shortage' January 29, 2014 http://www.bbc.com/news/education-25945413

Khallash, Sally: 'Top 10 global talent shortages' March 19, 2012 http://globaltalentstrategy.com/en/article/top-10-global-skills-shortages-105

Weisenthal, Joe: 'Here's The New Ranking Of Top Countries In Reading, Science, And Math' December 3, 2013 http://www.businessinsider.com/pisa-rankings-2013-12

'Skills shortage list' http://www.workpermit.com/australia/skills_shortage_list.htm

Foster, Karen: 'What's Good about Generation Y?' January 24, 2013 http://greatergood.berkeley.edu/article/item/whats_good_about_generation_y

'How to Develop Professional Expertise' http://www.wikihow.com/Develop-Professional-Expertise

'Heritability of IQ' April 8, 2014
http://en.wikipedia.org/wiki/Heritability_of_IQ

Coughlan, Sean: 'Shanghai teachers flown in for maths' March 11,
2014 http://www.bbc.com/news/education-26533428

Coughlan, Sean: 'Asians top of school tables – England in maths top
10' December 11, 2012 http://www.bbc.com/news/education-
20664752

'Why is numeracy important?'
http://www.nationalnumeracy.org.uk/why-is-numeracy-
important/index.html

'Teaching Through the Ages: Pictures of Famous Educators :
Discovery Channel' http://www.discovery.com/tv-
shows/curiosity/topics/famous-educators-pictures.htm

Zeidner, Moshe, Matthews, Gerald and Roberts, Richard D.: (2009)
'What We Know about Emotional Intelligence', Massachusetts
Institute of Technology

'Environmental Awareness Strategy 2011 – 2015' Environment
Directorate
http://www.giveorget.ie/upload/2011%20EARU%20Strategy.pdf

Albert, Jr. Gore: 'The Future: Six Drivers of Global Change' February
1, 2013 http://www.amazon.co.uk/Future-Six-Drivers-Global-
Change/dp/0812982894

Quick, Brin: 'Ways to Increase Public Awareness About Environmental
Problems' http://classroom.synonym.com/ways-increase-public-
awareness-environmental-problems-2590.html

'How to Help Save the Environment' http://www.wikihow.com/Help-
Save-the-Environment

'David Attenborough' March 8, 2014
http://en.wikipedia.org/wiki/David_Attenborough

'Al Gore' April 8, 2014 http://en.wikipedia.org/wiki/Al_Gore

'How to Exercise Your Brain' http://www.wikihow.com/Exercise-Your-Brain

Wells, Dr. Greg: 'Want to boost your brain power? Three ways getting physical can help' May 15, 2014
http://www.theglobeandmail.com/life/health-and-fitness/health-advisor/want-to-boost-your-brain-power-three-ways-getting-physical-can-help/article18680748/

Goleman, Daniel: 'Exercising the Mind to Treat Attention Deficits' May 12, 2014 http://well.blogs.nytimes.com/2014/05/12/exercising-the-mind-to-treat-attention-deficits/?_php=true&_type=blogs&_r=0

Joshua Freedman, 6 seconds, Nexus EQ.
http://www.6seconds.org/2013/05/29/third-decade-emotional-intelligence/

Jarvie, Michelle: 'Exercise your brain and improve your memory' May 5, 2014, Michigan State University
http://msue.anr.msu.edu/news/exercise_your_brain_and_improve_your_memory

'Brain Research Foundation Grant Expands Research on Using Exercise to Slow the Path to Alzheimer's and Dementia' May 15, 2014
http://www.digitaljournal.com/pr/1919471

Atkins, Joline Pinto: 'Exercise for the brain' May 11, 2014
http://www.timesonline.com/healthandwellness/shapeupwithjo/exercise-for-the-brain/article_5c3839c7-6372-52a0-b5ad-125bd2a253a0.html

http://www.businessballs.com/personalchangeprocess.htm

Ross, Elizabeth Kubler: '5 stages of grief model Kübler-Ross model' May 17, 2014 http://en.wikipedia.org/wiki/K%C3%BCbler-Ross_model

'Lessons from the Heart' http://www.pbs.org/bodyandsoul/203/heartmath.htm

Choo, Choon Sian: Getting a Permanent Change with Neuro Associative Conditioning (NAC) November 24, 2011 http://choonsian.blogspot.com/2011/11/getting-permanent-change-with-neuro.html

Tartakovsky, Margarita: 'How to Manage Emotions More Effectively' http://psychcentral.com/blog/archives/2012/07/03/how-to-manage-emotions-more-effectively/

'How to Gain Control of Your Emotions' http://www.wikihow.com/Gain-Control-of-Your-Emotions

Small, Russ: '5 Emotional Control Techniques' February 23, 2010 http://www.russellsmall.com/energy/5-emotional-control-techniques.html

'Managing Strong Emotions' http://www.colorado.edu/conflict/peace/treatment/angermgt.htm

Tartakovsky, Margarita: 'Techniques for Teens: How to Cope with Your Emotions' http://psychcentral.com/blog/archives/2013/07/20/techniques-for-teens-how-to-cope-with-your-emotions/

Wezowski, Patryk & Wezowski, Kasia: 'Emotional Management Method' http://www.emotionalmanagementmethod.com/about-us/

'Impact of Fear and Anxiety' http://www.takingcharge.csh.umn.edu/enhance-your-wellbeing/security/facing-fear/impact-fear

'Treat your brain right'
http://www.bbc.co.uk/scotland/brainsmart/brain/

Bergland, Christopher: 'Neuroscientists Discover How the Brain Learns While We Sleep' November 11, 2013
http://www.psychologytoday.com/blog/the-athletes-way/201311/neuroscientists-discover-how-the-brain-learns-while-we-sleep

'How the brain learns' http://projectflexner.sites.medinfo.ufl.edu/how-we-learn/

Ford, Donald J.: 'Content Development: How the Brain Learns' July 20, 2011 https://www.trainingindustry.com/content-development/articles/how-the-brain-learns.aspx

Inglis-Arkell, Esther: 'The chemicals that make you happy. No. Not those.' June 6, 2011 http://io9.com/5818371/the-chemicals-that-make-you-happy—no—not-those

Widrich, Leo: 'What Happens To Our Brains When We Exercise And How It Makes Us Happier'
http://www.fastcompany.com/3025957/work-smart/what-happens-to-our-brains-when-we-exercise-and-how-it-makes-us-happier

'Neurotransmitter' February 8, 2014
http://en.wikipedia.org/wiki/Neurotransmitter

'Brain Chemical Messengers'
http://www.teachhealth.com/chemmess.html

'The Happy Brain Chemicals' http://altered-states.net/barry/newsletter185/

'What are the physical effects of fear?'
http://www.sharecare.com/health/human-emotions/what-physical-effects-fear

Breuning, Loretta Graziano: 'Meet Your Happy Chemicals' 2012
http://www.innermammalinstitute.org/meet-your-happy-chemicals-
dopamine-endorphin-oxytocin-serotonin/

'The World 2040' Members' Report # 4/2004, Copenhagen Institute
for Futures Studies
http://www.cifs.dk/doc/medlemsrapporter/mr2004_4_en.pdf

Stockley, Simon: 'IED Fellow's Programme' Imperial College, London
https://www.jbs.cam.ac.uk/fileadmin/user_upload/research/centres/ac
celerate-cambridge/downloads/entrepreneurship-and-
entrepreneurial-behaviour.pdf

McGeachie, Susan & Parkinson, Sarah: 'Increased environmental
awareness: turning it into business opportunities'
http://www.pwc.com/ca/en/banking-capital-
markets/publications/increased-environmental-awareness-2008-04-en
.pdf

'World Population to 2030' United Nations Department of Economic
and Social Affairs/Population Division, New York (2004)
http://www.un.org/esa/population/publications/longrange2/WorldPop
2300final.pdf

Fisher, John: 'The Process of Transition' (2012)
http://www.businessballs.com/personalchangeprocess.htm

Eager, Clare: 'The Emotion of Change', Chartered Management
Institute, People HR
http://www.peoplehr.co.uk/assets/PeopleHRPPTheEmotionofChangeF
eb11V2.pdf

http://www.brainyquote.com/

THE AUTHOR

Leeann C. Naidoo is a seasoned management consultant and executive coach, having worked for major consultancy firms such as Ernst & Young, Deloitte, Capgemini and PricewaterhouseCoopers, in the UK, the UAE and South Africa. A specialist in large scale and complex organisational change and transformation, Leeann has worked across various industries and business sectors to deliver sustainable results in an accelerated way. Drawing on this experience, Leeann works with CEOs, business professionals, small business owners, women and students from around the world, helping them achieve personal excellence. She is a keynote speaker, on topics such as Mind Mastery, Emotional Intelligence, Entrepreneurial Behaviours, and Building Resilience. She lectures and coaches at major universities in South Africa. Leeann's company, Concordia Coaching, Consulting & Communications www.concordia-coaching.com, is a platform from which high impact, innovative neuroscience based techniques are taught to clients wanting to achieve personal excellence in their careers and their lives.

Leeann believes that creating a powerful mind-set will create a paradigm shift in the world, eradicating poverty, curing diseases, saving the forests, conserving wildlife and getting people to care more about the sanctity of life. She supports several charities around the world that share this vision. Leeann is 'retired' in South Africa with her husband and dogs.

If you are committed to making a change in your life, download your free Mind Age™ support pack from www.themindage.com.